LENT
A TIME FOR RENEWAL
S E R M O N   B O O K

Lenten Studies, Sermons, and Worship Resources
for Ash Wednesday to Easter

Gerhard Aho • Donald Deffner • Richard Kapfer

Unless otherwise noted, the Scripture quotations in this publication are from *The Holy Bible: NEW INTERNATIONAL VERSION,* © 1973, 1978, 1984 by the International Bible Society. Used by permission of Zondervan Bible Publishers.

Copyright © 1989 Concordia Publishing House
3558 S. Jefferson Avenue, St. Louis, MO 63118-3968
Manufactured in the United States of America

1 2 3 4 5 6 7 8 9 10   98 97 96 95 94 93 92 91 90 89

Contents

Part II: Sermons   Donald L. Deffner

Part III: Worship Resources   Richard G. Kapfer

Foreword

Lent is a time for renewal, or it serves no purpose at all. Lent is not a time for breast-beating, nor simply for reciting once again the history of the Passion. If that were all that Lent accomplished, it would be better to cancel Lenten services this year!

Lent has to do with repentance and renewal. It is a time when God's Spirit forces us to face who we are and what we have done, when God's Word breaks into our hearts with the message that we aren't meant to live as slaves of evil. Further, the message of repentance includes the cleansing power of the cross, which turns us around to face who we are in Jesus Christ and to see who and what we can become by His grace, power, and indwelling. That "becoming" is what this series is about, for the forgiven, restored, and renewed Christian has wonderful work to do. The components of this Lenten series describe the renewal that can, by God's power and blessing, be accomplished in us.

The faithful parish pastor longs for renewal of his congregation. We think of those who rarely worship and commune. We agonize over those whose love for the Savior has grown lukewarm. We remember those who teeter on the edge of doubt or despair. And we think of our own spiritual lives, for we too can become "weary of well-doing."

With these thoughts in mind, Lent can never be just the usual. It presents a real opportunity for growth in our congregation. Once we have carefully examined the themes of this series, all of which focus on the particular needs of every Christian and every parish, exciting possibilities present themselves. We can invite parishioners to attend the Lenten services because we want them to share in the renewal that the services highlight. We can visit the straying and delinquent, for what they need above all else is to be renewed. We can share the Lenten series with the unchurched in every possible way, for we have what they desperately need—renewal of life. This is why this series is titled *Lent: A Time for Renewal*. We believe that it is a timely, important series that can bring many blessings to many people.

Introduction

The title of the Lenten series suggests some directions for our preliminary thoughts.

A time. The Bible makes much of *kairos* (time). It is often used in the ordinary sense of a unit of measure—days, weeks, years—and to designate seasons or generations. In other instances *kairos* designates a completion, a fullness, an appointment that must be made or has been made. "The time has come. The kingdom of God is near" (Mark 1:15). ". . . until the times of the Gentiles are fulfilled" (Luke 21:24). "When the time had fully come . . ." (Gal. 4:4). In other instances *time* takes on the element of pressure, of urgency, of moments that must be grasped: "I tell you, now is the time of God's favor" (2 Cor. 6:2). As will become clear in each of the Lenten topics, *time* as used in the title has to do with (1) time in the Lenten season (a most appropriate time to think of repentance and renewal), (2) time in terms of fullness and completion (for everything is ready!), and (3) time in terms of urgency (about what needs renewing and cannot be ignored or delayed).

Renewal. Renewal suggests that something once was new, but over time and through misuse (or lack of use) it has become worn out, faded, and old. It is somewhat like working on a piece of furniture and discovering beautiful oak under layers of paint and varnish—the furniture was basically good; it simply was not cared for or appreciated. It needed to be *renewed,* brought back to its original condition. Each of the topics under consideration in this Lenten series treats an aspect of the renewed Christian life. Servanthood, obedience, witness, true religion, priorities, godly fear, unity, faith, and hope are always timely topics. *We,* not the topics, get worn down, covered with thickening coats of discouragement or carelessness, faded under the scorching sun of living in a hostile world.

A Time for Renewal also suggests our approach to the elements in this series. In each one we shall examine what needs renewing and scrape off the layers of sin and selfishness by looking at them through the words and actions of Jesus. We will be asking the vital question: If this is how we are meant to look and live, what went wrong? This will be followed by the obvious question: How can we be restored and renewed? Finally, we'll be asking: What does one look like when renewal has begun (for renewal is always happening and is never complete this side of heaven)? Hovering over all of this will be the *kairos,* the ticking of the clock that adds urgency to the task, and *charis,* the redemptive time found in Jesus Christ, who gives power and joy to the task.

LENT
A Time for Renewal

SERMON STUDIES

Lent: A Time for Renewal of Servanthood

Whoever wants to become great among you must be your servant. (Matt. 20:26)

John 13:1–17

Introduction

Servanthood is a word that can easily get caught in the throat. All of us know what servanthood is in its usual sense—one person serving another unselfishly and cheerfully. But servanthood as a way of life? Servanthood as the opposite of lordship? All the time? Finding our purpose and meaning in life through servanthood? With no reservations, no limitations, no time off?

We can avoid the sting of servanthood by talking in generalities or by talking of its opposite—lordship—without ever facing servanthood in its radical demand on our lives and its searching look at our assumptions. In this way, we can condemn lordship, exalt service in general, say the Good News, and end the sermon quickly.

But Jesus' actions and words will not be avoided. He "poured water into a basin and began to wash his disciples' feet, drying them with the towel that was wrapped around him" (John 13:5). When He had finished, He said, "I have set you an example that you should do as I have done for you" (v. 15).

The Word

We are introduced to this word in a moment of embarrassment that led to anger. The subject wasn't servanthood. It was lordship. The mother of Zebedee's sons, James and John, sought out Jesus when He was at a convenient distance from the other disciples. She got on her knees while her sons stood on either side, heads down, sandaled feet drawing nervous pictures in the sand. "Psst! Jesus! I have a request. Command that one of these two sons of mine sit at your right hand and the other at your left in your kingdom" (cf. Matt. 20:21).

Apparently, Mrs. Zebedee sensed that something was going to happen to Jesus, and it was going to be big. Before He got too busy, she put in an embarrassed request for her sons. After all, it's not *what* you know but *who,* and the *who* was Jesus, who would bring in a kingdom much bigger than anything anyone could imagine.

Jesus answered clearly and loudly enough for the others to hear and understand, and they became angry. They too had visions of the future. Their minds were made up—so made up that Jesus' words predicting His death (Matt. 20:17–19) had not penetrated. They were kingdom seekers, and what He had said didn't fit with their visions of the kingdom.

Some observations are in order:

1. All 12 disciples, plus the mother of James and John, without any formal prior discussion of the subject among them, had an identical vision of the kingdom.

2. Their vision of the kingdom did not match Jesus' vision.

3. The problem with Mrs. Zebedee and the Twelve wasn't that they were looking for a high position. It was that they were looking in the wrong place.

The first point tells us something important. Most people, including Christian people (when they aren't in a church setting where certain answers are expected), will agree that rulership is a major goal of life. One could argue that this rulership isn't meant to be nasty—like that of a tyrant. Zebedee's sons didn't have that in mind. But they *did* want the rulership that *power* gives, and so did the other disciples. They were working with a "given" of life. That is the major problem that Jesus confronts here—the assumption that having power over others is the way things ought to be—or if not *ought* to be, it is at least the way things are.

Think of the power plays that take place among people in your own congregation—between children and parents; between spouses; on the job, off the job in friendly social gatherings; between the young man and woman in your office contemplating marriage; between the sexes; between pastor and members of boards. Somehow, we seem to need "pecking orders" that require dominating and subjugated personalities.

It's instructive that the Twelve had no problem with rulership. They agreed that someone should rule (under Jesus, of course). The argument came only in sorting out *who* should rule. If a vote were taken, each disciple would have received one vote—as people would in family squabbles, marital squabbles, office squabbles, and church squabbles.

The Action

That brings us to Maundy Thursday. It's a few days removed from the scene described above. The words of Jesus still hadn't penetrated. Now they were all in the Upper Room to celebrate the Passover. Since there were only the Twelve plus Jesus, somebody had to take on the servant's role, for their feet had to be washed before eating. Nobody moved. The food was getting cold. The one who moved would be the doormat, the fool, the loser. The servant would give up forever his claim to rulership over the others. (So they sit in your office, arms folded, looking away from each other, saying nothing, for they know as well as you that someone has to speak, someone has to give in, and giving in means failure, admission of guilt, humiliation, contempt, and "losing.") Finally, someone *did* move. He took towel and basin, knelt down, and began washing their feet.

Perhaps we need to equip our offices with fewer crosses and more towels and basins. Maybe instead of fish symbols on our doors and crosses on the walls of our homes we need pictures of feet and hands and a towel and basin. It's too bad Albrecht Dürer painted praying hands; maybe wet hands would have been better. And maybe we ought to have drills on how to use towels and basins, much like learning CPR.

The disciples, no doubt, were ashamed of themselves. Peter's spoken reaction probably represented the others' thoughts. Perhaps on other occasions, had events proceeded as usual, they would have agreed to wash each other's feet—that is, if no one else was looking in who hadn't heard the words of Jesus, lest they get the wrong idea; if they didn't have to do it every time; if the others took their turns; and if there was a payoff, a reason, like doing such a good job that they would be elevated to where someone else would wash their feet in the kingdom of this world.

The Hard Word and Action

So we have the *words* of Jesus (Matt. 20:26) and the *action* of Jesus (John 13:3–11) that point to how we *ought* to be. The words and actions tell us that rulership is to be sought not in power plays and ruling over the others but in serving others. Service is demonstrated with a towel and basin and bended knees.

What we ought to be is clear. *How* we ought to be is clear. The "what" and the "how" come straight from God. But our sinful nature has a hard time with servanthood.

It's silly to take the risk of being foot washers for others, especially if they don't appreciate it. It's costly to be a foot washer for a family in need, for a friend who is suffering, for a child who misuses us. It's easier to wait and let someone else do it. It's far more pleasant to be served than to serve, to be noticed, to be appreciated. What is more, there is little pressure to become foot washers. The pressure is from the other direction; we want to be served.

A few years ago a Bible study produced by an independent group dealt with the theme of servanthood. It examined the servant from many aspects— slave, table waiter, helper, etc. The problem with the study—and the main reason we chose not to use it—is that it approached servanthood entirely from the direction of the Law. That's not enough. The commands of the Law can only create guilt. The "oughts" and "thou shalts" of Scripture do not take away our weakness and sin. If Lent is to be a time of renewal, it must say more than what we ought to do. It must bring us to Jesus Christ, who didn't stop with "ought."

The disciples didn't really understand foot washing. For them the kingdom remained a kingdom of power and glory. When Jesus came into their lives during their days of discipleship, He opened to them worlds they never knew existed. But what did they see? They apparently saw a king who would rule by feeding hungry people, a religious high priest who would rule through religion, a healer who would rule through quick cures. In spite of many opportunities and occasional insights (Matt. 16:17; John. 6:68–69), they kept thinking of earthly kingdoms and earthly power (see Acts 1:6) until the day of Pentecost. The key to understanding servanthood does not come from sharing words about it or seeing demonstrations of it. It comes from a whole new heart, a renewed heart.

The Servant

Why was Jesus *doing* it? Why was *He* washing feet? Why was He here (in the Upper Room, in this world) anyway? John tells us: "Jesus knew that the Father had put all things under his power, and that he had come from God and was returning to God; so he got up from the meal, took off his outer clothing . . ." (John 13:3-4).

Jesus knew where He came from, where He was going, and who He was taking with Him. If you know where you came from and where you are going, you will live differently in between, in the present.

The world says that you came from nowhere and that you are going nowhere, so make the most of now by taking your share. One of the "sons of thunder," John, learned better and wrote: "Do not love the world or anything in the world. If anyone loves the world, the love of the Father is not in him. For everything in the world—the cravings of sinful man, the lust of his eyes and the boasting of what he has and does—comes not from the Father but from the world. The world and its desires pass away, but the man who does the will of God lives forever" (1 John 2:15–17). John received more than the words and actions of Jesus in foot washing. He was linked by faith to the Servant Jesus in all that He had come to do. (Isaiah 53 has much to say about Him as servant.)

Servant Jesus bent down from heaven to earth to wash us clean from sin. The One crowned with thorns comes to crown us as children of the kingdom. The naked One comes to place on us the robes of righteousness. The crucified Christ rises from the grave to free us from the world's deadness and to give us a new vision of life and greatness.

As a sign of the kingdom and a down payment on what awaits us, He hands us a towel and basin, saying, "You are a child of the new kingdom, and in you the new age has come. Go and be servants in My name. This is what life is about."

Christ's Servants Renewed

What does this look like? Here you can fill out the description, but we suggest a few:

- Parents and children who serve each other *not* just because they are parents and children, but because they live in the kingdom.
- A Christian congregation that becomes a community of care, a haven from selfishness, a place where people serve each other in love.
- Husbands and wives who are subject to each other out of reverence for Christ.

Servanthood looks like Jesus, bending down into our lives, taking the form of a servant, and loving us, even to the point of death on the cross.

Servanthood looks like you and me, people who by nature would like to be lords and masters, receiving the honor and service of others, but people who remember, repent, and are renewed, knowing that "whoever wants to become great among you must be your servant"—and servants of Servant Jesus.

Sermon Outline

Introduction: It will be necessary to spend the first few moments of this first sermon in the series introducing the concept of time (see Introduction, page 00) and the general theme for the Lenten series. Then introduce the subject of servanthood, perhaps in this way: The mother of James and John came to Jesus with a solemn request, not one involving her sons and servanthood but one that asked that they be given positions of rulership. In a reversal of our theme, her request begins us on a journey in time that leads us into

Outline :   Lent: A Time for Renewal of Servanthood
  I. Servanthood isn't acceptable in our world
      A. Because of our natural striving for rulership
      B. Because of our natural desire for power
 II. Jesus rejected earthly power
      A. By His words about rulership
      B. By His action of foot washing
      C. But this rejection alone does not suffice or help
III. How could Jesus—and we—stoop so low?
      A. It has to do with who He is and what He did.
          1. He came to kneel in humble service to us.
          2. His greatest service was His death—in service to us.
      B. It has to do with who we are because of Servant Jesus.
          1. Jesus' service has given us eternal honor and riches.
          2. We are new creatures, free to serve our neighbor.

Conclusion: Where should this renewal of servanthood begin? It may need to begin in your home, in your marriage, in your place of work. But most important, it must begin at the cross. Then let it happen from the cross through you, for Jesus Himself will hand you the towel and basin. He will point you to where you should go. Most important, He will go with you.

Lent 2

Lent: A Time for Renewal of Obedience

*Humble yourselves, therefore, under God's mighty hand,
that he may lift you up in due time. (1 Peter 5:6)*

Mark 14:32–42

What Theological Functions Does the Text Perform?

A. How does the Law reveal the human situation apart from God?
The exhortation to humble ourselves reminds us that there is in all of us a
pride that rebels against God. Yet rebellion is futile because God's hand is
mighty. God is ultimately the decisive power in the world, and His work
cannot be hampered or destroyed. We may think that we are resisting and
thwarting God's work, but we only appear to do so. Pride, self-interest, and
self-exaltation, however futile, drive out God's Spirit from the heart and
quench whatever blessed work He may have done.

In 1 Peter 5:5 the Greek word that is translated "clothe" could refer to
the garb of slaves, which was also their badge of service and a sign of their
station and duty. It is not enough that we wear the garment of low-mind-
edness; we are also to put on the badge of menial service. Slaves were
expected to obey their master unquestioningly. Similarly, we are to obey
God without question, letting God's hand assign us to the proper service
of others.

In his exhortation Peter counters our tendency to build castles of conceit,
to regard servile dress as unsuitable, and to insist on our claims rather than
responding to another's claims on us. This exhortation reminds us of our
proud resistance to God's clear commands, of our complaining under God-
sent crosses, and of our depreciation of others. Without God's gracious
action in us, we remain proud, for humility is foreign to our selfish nature.
We would rather be on top and receive homage.

In affliction we are by nature inclined to rebel against God and to judge
God's actions. We are not born willing to trust Him, to believe that He
knows what is best for us. God's ways and will seem much too hard for us,
and our own wisdom would take the easy way out.

B. How does the Gospel reveal God's gracious nature and action?
The Gospel message of the text is that God exalts the humble. God has
already exalted us by Christ's humble death for us. We have been lifted up,
born again to a living hope, through the resurrection of Jesus Christ from
the dead. We are "a chosen people, a royal priesthood, a holy nation, people
belonging to God" (2:9). We are brothers and sisters of Jesus (Matt. 12:50).

Exaltation will come in due time on the last great day, when we are crowned with glory and honor and see Christ as He is.

C. What response is God, through Law and Gospel, seeking to evoke from the readers or hearers?

God wants us to humble ourselves—to recognize our unworthiness before Him and thus see ourselves as we really are. We also humble ourselves when we submit in patient resignation to God's will and ways. When we see ourselves as sinners, we will not be so ready to blow our own trumpet or to hear others sing our praises. Recognizing our need of God's grace, we will also be in a position to receive it. Relying on God's gift of His Son and His Spirit, we are free to search out the good of others, willingly putting on the garment that proclaims our servanthood.

God enables us to anticipate our final exaltation by giving us, even in our struggles and work of service, an exaltation that is already ours by faith in Christ. This anticipation helps us to live in obedience to God and as slaves to one another as Christ was to us. Our service to one another is the evidence of our obedience and of the overflowing fruit of God's service to us.

How Does the Language of the Text Convey Law and Gospel?

A. Word meanings that provide cues for Law and Gospel.

Humble (*tapeinoō*). In the active voice the verb means to make low or to abase. Here, in the passive, it means to submit, to lower oneself, to let oneself be humbled, to accept one's humiliation. The implication is that we are to be on guard against an overbearing and haughty spirit. We are to show respect and consideration also for the poor and lowly, for those who seem inferior to us and who may even be ungrateful for our service. Humility shows itself in scrupulous obedience to God and in patient resignation to His will. Christ in Gethsemane is the supreme example. His humility in service is a model for us. If the Son of God, possessing all power and glory, could for our sake lower Himself to death on a cross, can we not lower ourselves by willingly serving one another?

Under (*hupo*). We may try, but we can never exalt ourselves above God. He remains the high, the great, the holy One, despite our supposed power and accomplishments. In Him we live and move and have our being, and therefore we are always under Him.

Mighty (*krateios*). God possesses all power and controls all things, the universe and all that is in it. What God sends we cannot and will not escape. That can strike fear, but it is also reassuring, for God is mighty enough to deliver and sustain us, no matter what we go through.

Hand (*cheir*). God's hand of power shows itself in His mighty acts of creation and redemption, in the resurrection of Jesus Christ, and in making people spiritually alive.

Exalt (*hupsoō*). God, who will one day bless us before His judgment seat by calling us the blessed of the Father and receiving us into His heavenly kingdom, has already now raised us up to sit with Christ in the heavenly places (Eph. 2:6).

Time (*kairos*). The reference here is to the end time. The apostle uses our future exaltation to motivate us to accept our present humiliation. Yet already at this time God is exalting us who are humbled under His mighty hand. Besides assuring us of our high station in Christ, God lets us experience the inner peace and patience that come from confidence in His hand of power and peace. There is exaltation in the character development God brings about.

B. Grammar and syntax that serve as facilitators of Law and Gospel.
The imperative mode in the opening exhortation tells us not only that we have a responsibility but that we can discipline ourselves to be humble. We can do so because in Christ we are already new people. We will therefore strive to have the same attitude that Christ had (Phil. 2:5).

The accusative case after *hupo* indicates being under power, rule, sovereignty. Think of the warning and reassurance implicit here.

The purpose clause introduced by *hina* shows the Gospel-oriented purpose of humbling ourselves. This can also be taken as a result clause.

"In due time" (dative expressing time) here refers to the end time when God will gloriously exalt us.

C. Rhetorical devices that point to Law or Gospel.
God's "hand" is an anthropomorphism suggesting God's power, which no one can overthrow. That same power works for the protection of His own.

In 1 Peter 5:5, the aorist imperative *enkombōsasthe* refers to putting on a garment that must be tied on. This could be the apron of slaves, which was fastened to the girdle of the vest. This garment showed the station of the slave as servant. Peter is probably thinking here also of the slave's *lention* or towel, which Christ used when He washed His disciples' feet (John 13:4). As Christ's own servants, we are to wear the clothing that announces us as slaves, the garment of humility, which is the livery of His household. Furthermore, this clothing is to be habitually worn by us.

How Do Polarities in the Text Suggest Law and Gospel?

Polarity lies in humility, with pride as its opposite. Law and Gospel are encompassed also in the humbling and the exalting. God reveals our pride in the form of false humility. God humbles us with His Law. Through the good news of the Gospel He exalts us, bringing us to faith in Christ and to a participation in all the blessings Christ earned for us.

How Do Correlates in the Text and/or Context Express Law and Gospel?

Humbling and exalting function also as correlates. God, by means of the Law, humbles us so that we recognize and acknowledge our smallness and

His greatness. God exalts us by clothing us in Christ's holiness, goodness, and beauty. The imperative of the text is clearly Law, laying on us the responsibility to recognize our creatureliness. At the same time, the Gospel (in the exalting) reminds us that God lifts us up. We are, already in this life, lifted up to a life that is connected to Christ above (Col. 3:1–4) so that our struggles and service do not overcome our joy and confidence.

Humbling ourselves in obedience to God's will and in conformity with God's commands also requires effort and resolution on our part. But this obedience, required by the Law, must be correlated with the power of the Gospel contained in the promise of God's exaltation.

Correlation of Law and Gospel may be seen in God's "mighty hand" in contrast to our weak hand or in God's controlling hand in contrast to Satan's weakened hand.

Another correlate: Sinful pride (e.g., false humility), of which the Law makes us aware while the Gospel empowers us to show proper humility.

What Is the Gospel Perspective of the Text?

The Gospel perspective is that Christ humbled Himself all the way to death on a cross to exalt us, that we might be children of God and heirs of heaven. Our station is an exalted one, but only through Christ and in Christ. Our present exaltation guarantees our future exaltation, which will be greater than anything we can imagine.

Because of Jesus we can live now with humility—the humility that acknowledges Christ's greatness rather than our own. The greatness of Christ showed itself above all in His willingness to serve us even to death. He was willing to obey His heavenly Father because He wanted to save us. Our humility also expresses itself in obedience to God, in willingness to carry out God's will. We can expect to suffer here, but God exalts us and will exalt us as He has exalted Christ.

Sermon Outline

Introduction: Bitter was the cup Jesus began drinking in Gethsemane—the cup of vain thoughts, cruel words, evil deeds; the cup of violence and injustice; the cup of human rebellion against God and disobedience to His will. No wonder Jesus asked that this cup be removed! "Yet not what I will, but what you will" (Mark 14:36). As He had always been obedient to His Father, so now, although the cup's anguish was intense and would get worse as He bore sin's punishment, He would nevertheless bow to His Father's will. Jesus would obey.

In our emphasis on the grace and love of God we sometimes forget that we are to obey God. We are to do what He commands and avoid what He forbids. The Christian life is not only comforts and thrills, exciting worship in God's house, and unexpected help in trouble. It is a life of daily obedience.

Peter equates obeying God with humbling ourselves under God's mighty hand. Peter's words point us to

Outline :   Lent: A Time for Renewal of Obedience

I. Obedience to God is often hard for us.
  A. It requires the garment of humility.
    1. We don't like the servant role.
    2. We don't like to subject ourselves to each other.
  B. God's ways appear too demanding.
    1. Peter's readers endured suffering they couldn't always understand (1 Peter 5:9–10).
    2. Christ's suffering was excruciatingly hard to bear (Mark 14:36).
    3. We don't always understand why we must suffer.
  C. Our disobedience shows up in various ways.
    1. Finding it hard to submit humbly to God's guidance, we rebel against the course of events and try to resist and thwart His might.
    2. Forgetting that His mighty hand is leading us, we question His ways with us.
    3. We are tempted simply to choose to do what God has clearly forbidden.

II. Obedience to God is possible for us.
  A. Because God has already exalted us.
    1. The way to our exaltation is opened when we humbly confess our sin. Then we are ready to receive what God wishes to give us.
    2. Our exaltation came through what Jesus did for us in the suffering that began in Gethsemane and climaxed on the cross.
    3. Our obedience flows from the love we have for God, who exalted us in Christ while we were yet sinners.
  B. Because God will exalt us in due time.
    1. God's time for supremely exalting us will come on the last great day. Then we will receive an unfading crown of glory.
    2. Then we shall experience fully what it means to sit with Christ in the heavenly places (Eph. 2:6) as righteous and royal children of God.

Conclusion: God's exalting of us in Christ empowers us to humble ourselves before God in obedience to His will. It's good to know that we live and move under His almighty hand.

Sermon Illustrations

There are two familiar hymns that begin with the words: "Awake, my soul, stretch every nerve, And press with vigour on." The other, even more famous, was written a century before by Bishop Ken, and it runs: "Awake, my soul, and with the sun, Thy daily stage of duty run." These are two contrasting moods, and each profoundly Christian. Both suggest a way of beginning the day, a kind of getting-up prayer as we roll out of bed and stretch our limbs. The one—"Awake, my soul, stretch every nerve, And press with vigour on"—is a kind of trumpet-call to action, a summons to the thrill and adventure of the Christian life. The other—designed perhaps for those who don't like trumpet-calls at 7:30 a.m.—contains a very plain reminder that the Christian life is also a matter of ordinary Christian duty. . . .

This is worth thinking about. Have we got into the habit of romanticizing the Christian life, . . . we would want to change the couplet: . . . "Awake, my soul, and with the sun, Let's have more light and health and fun." That's the picture—excitement, energy, happiness, surprise—and we are quite right in believing that this is part of the Christian life. But it is not the whole of it, and we do well to listen again to the old bishop: "Awake, my soul, and with the sun, Thy daily stage of duty run." For in fact the Christian life is just as much a matter of "daily duty" as it is of comforts and thrills.

David H. C. Read, *I Am Persuaded* (Charles Scribner's Sons, 1961), pp. 64–65

One company commander was as hard-nosed as they come. He was firm and rigid. He had come up through the ranks, and the First Sergeant demeanor never left him. . . . If there seemed to be no clear-cut rule, he made one up, and gigged men on inspection for failure to meet *his* standards. He had more men on company restriction than all the other units of the post combined. And he also had a frightful number of men departing without official leave. He was a tyrant, and everyone knew it.

The other commander was tough on his men too. He commanded with authority, but he spoke with gentleness. He respected his men, and they respected him. He maintained excellent discipline, but there was seldom need to punish his soldiers, and never did any go AWOL.

The Law without Jesus is a tyrant, similar to the first commander I mentioned. The Law *with* grace in Christ is similar to the second. There is a proper balance. John tells us, "This is the love of God, that we keep His commandments. And," he observes, "His commandments are not burdensome."

Richard Andersen, "Take On the Whole World," *The Concordia Pulpit for 1976* (CPH, 1975), p. 140.

Israel stood at Kadesh-Barnea (Num. 13), on the fringe of the land of promise, with blessed memories of God's providence and assurances of His power to lead them victoriously into this inheritance. He had said the land was theirs. He had said, "Go up and possess it." But the word of the Lord was not enough. The divine imperative was subjected to a human franchise. The attitude was not, "Let's take a step of faith, and believe God's promise." It was rather, "surely [the land] floweth with milk and honey . . . *nevertheless* . . ." And the results were catastrophic. A whole generation missed its destiny, wandering in the wilderness. The sorry episode has been repeated many times, in national and individual life. God has spoken, made His will known beyond doubt, but our wills have resisted Him and the result has been our immense loss.

Wilbur E. Nelson, *Anecdotes and Illustrations* (Baker, 1971), pp. 10–11.

A man reported not long ago that he was startled by an unusual reference to Sunday. In a little book entitled *Business Laws in Daily Use* there was this statement, "Contracts made on Sunday cannot be enforced." That gave a jolt to his mind. He said, "Many contracts made on Sunday are not enforced on weekdays." Not that they *cannot* be, but they *are* not. Worship is not a contract, of course, but it is often an implied covenant. It inspires high aspirations, determinations, pledges for the future. Then in the rush of the weeks and months, often they are not enforced. Someone has said, "Whenever I am moved to take exercise, I lie down until the feeling has passed." Too many people do that in regard to the Christian covenant they have made.

Nelson, p. 28.

A woman had suffered a lot of agony over her daughter's unfulfilled life. The suffering the daughter had gone through she made her own. But the painful identification with her girl's difficulties had not subsided until she came to the realization, as she put it: "Two weeks ago I finally gave up on worrying about my daughter's problems. I finally turned them over to God. I said, 'Here, God, you take over. I can't handle it any more.' " That was obedience—in resignation to God. That was looking unto Him in all things and knowing He is able to do that which we are unable to do. At this moment that mother has seen no immediate change in her girl's life. But the mother has an inner peace she didn't have before, for she learned to obey Christ's words: "If you love me keep my commandment . . ." the commandment to "cast all your cares on me, for I care for you . . ."

Donald L. Deffner, *Bound to be Free* (Morse Press, 1981), p. 88.

Many Christians feel worthless because, I'm convinced, they don't understand humility. Humility is not "being made humble before the Lord" until you have lost all self-respect. Losing self-respect leads not to mature but to masochistic sainthood (if there is such a thing). I wonder—do we mistake a martyr-like, sacrificial, masochistic attitude toward the Lord as enlightened? True humility is none of these.

Humility in the Bible means taking a true evaluation of yourself—of your virtues too. If you're good at something, then take credit for it, recognize it. Don't say, "Really now, it was nothing." It was something. It was God's grace showing in your life. It was the light of the world coming through.

There's just as much pride showing on your part by not taking the credit when you should as when you shouldn't but do. How good are you at receiving a compliment? Pride can wear a many-colored garment. It has a large wardrobe.

This is the beauty, though, and the power of justification: to be justified before God means we can now stand before our Creator without an inferiority complex, delivered from false humility. The cross did a wonderful thing when it killed pride dressed up in all its manifestations. We're free, church. We don't have to wring our hands or sweat it out anymore. That's true freedom. And that's true humility.

Lynn Ridenhour, *Seasonings for Sermons,* vol. 2 (CSS, 1982), p. 11.

A young man just out of the Army was interviewed for a job. "What did you do in the service?" the interviewer asked him. The young man replied, "As told."

Phil Barnhart, *Seasonings for Sermons* (CSS, 1980), p. 122

Obedience makes sense when you understand that this obedience will get you into trouble. You obey the speed limit when to disobey may get you arrested. You observe the IRS regulations; if you don't, you pay a fine. It can be demonstrated that to disobey the commandments, "Thou shalt not kill," "Thou shalt not steal," "Thou shalt not commit adultery," is to invite all sorts of unpleasantness.

There's another kind of obedience that does not rest on understanding at all. It rests on trust. This is the kind God asks of us. We don't honor God very much by not killing someone; it simply doesn't pay. But when we obey God in matters that we cannot understand or that have every chance of giving us trouble—that's obedience out of sheer trust. We honor God most by this kind of obedience. When they were small, my boys were quite different. One, when I asked him to do something, would irk me by asking, "Why?" The other didn't bother to ask; he simply went ahead and did it. I suppose I should have been pleased with the curiosity and caution of the first son, but I confess I was more pleased with the second—with his obedience and trust.

God cannot be displeased when his children try to find out why they ought to do something he has asked. But he has asked us to do many things where there are no obvious reasons.

Alvin N. Rogness, *The Word for Every Day* (Augsburg, 1981), p. 35.

Lent: A Time for Renewal of Witness

Whoever acknowledges me before men, I will also acknowledge him before my Father in heaven. But whoever disowns me before men, I will disown him before my Father in heaven. (Matt. 10:32–33)

Mark 14:66–72

General Setting of the Text

A characteristic of Matthew's gospel is the application of Old Testament prophecies to the childhood, public ministry, and final sufferings of Jesus. Matthew attaches prophetic oracles as labels to events that Mark simply reports as matters of fact. Thus Mark's flat statement, "They went to Capernaum" (Mark 1:21), referring to Christ and His followers proceeding north from the scene of His baptism, takes on in Matthew the character of a solemn announcement of an event in which is fulfilled the prophecy of a great light in Galilee of the Gentiles. Similarly, Mark's matter-of-fact account of the extensive healing ministry in Capernaum (Mark 1:23–34) contrasts with Matthew's citation in connection with the healings of Isaiah's prophecy about the Suffering Servant of God (Matt. 8:17). Again, Mark states simply that Jesus withdrew to the sea after His discussion with the Pharisees (Mark 3:7), while Matthew attaches to this withdrawal a prophecy of what the Messiah would be like (Matt. 12:15–21). Matthew thus enriches his account of Christ's life for purposes of apologetics and edification. Throughout the Gospel Matthew shows that Jesus possessed the qualities for messiahship. He thereby wishes to confirm Jewish Christians in the faith that Jesus is the Christ.

Immediate Context

The unit of thought immediately preceding the text comprises verses 24–31. In verses 24–25 Jesus reminds the disciples that if He, their teacher and master, is being persecuted and hated by the world, they will not escape that hatred either. But the disciples should have no fear of what people do to them (v. 26). Christ is mighty enough to protect them. Besides, the message they are proclaiming will become known throughout the world, although Christ's ministry and that of the disciples is still relatively obscure and hidden at this time. Now they are still speaking the Gospel "in the dark," which probably refers to Christ's instruction within the intimate group of the disciples (v. 27). But the time will come when the Gospel will be uttered in the light, that is, in the open. What is now being "whispered," that is, spoken in the intimate, familiar group, will be preached "from the roofs," publicly proclaimed before the world. Although the wider proclamation will bring more hostility, it should also encourage the disciples to further the cause of the kingdom even more.

Another reason for them not to give way to fear is advanced in verses 28–31. The disciples need to keep in mind that they are under the protective providence of God. Not only their lives but even the hair of their heads is under the protection of God's hand. He cares for the very least; He even protects the sparrow. So there is no need to fear. People may kill them, but that is all they can do. God alone has the power to cast into hell. The disciples are of absolute worth to God. Therefore, they can go about their work without fear, despite the hatred and threats of those who oppose the Gospel. This thought leads into the text, which emphasizes that on His glorious return Jesus will confess every faithful witness before the Father and before His angels.

The unit of thought immediately following the text (vv. 34–36) emphasizes that the consequences of the confession of Jesus in human affairs will be discord, strife, and conflict even within intimate family circles. Although Jesus is the Prince of Peace, who came to establish peace between God and humanity and among people, and who fills the hearts of His believers with peace, this purpose will be attained only through the suppression of sin and its consequences. But the overthrow of sin and its power results in conflict. Individuals will either be for Christ or against Him, and that division will affect relationships even within families. In this respect Christ came not to bring peace but a sword. In verses 37–39 Jesus points out that a person must be prepared to give up even what is nearest and dearest; all must be sacrificed for the sake of Christ. Christ demands a devotion that exceeds even what we owe to our next of kin. Those who love family members more than Christ, and avoid suffering for Christ's sake to save the lives of their family as well as themselves, will lose them for eternity. But Christians who are ready to suffer and to sacrifice everything, even their lives, for Christ's sake will find eternal life.

Text in the Vernacular

Verse 33: The KJV, NAS, TEV, and Beck have "whoever will confess," while the NIV, NEB, RSV, and Phillips have "acknowledge." Phillips, NEB, and NIV use "disowns"; other English translations have "whoever confesses" and "whoever denies me." TEV has "whoever confesses publicly that he belongs to me" and "whoever denies publicly that he belongs to me."

Text in the Original

In verse 32, *homologēsei en emoi* is an Aramaic idiom that translates literally "shall confess in me." In verse 33, the preposition is omitted and the accusatives *me* and *auton* are used: "deny me," "deny him." To confess in Christ is to speak and live in a manner that agrees with Christ. Christ in turn will confess that person before the Father and will Himself dwell in the person who has embraced Him by faith. The confession that is made of

Christ agrees with His person, work, and teaching. The true confessor has unity with Christ and Christ with the confessor. The future tense, *homologēsō,* points particularly to Judgment Day, when Jesus will acknowledge the believer before the eternal Father, who is Lord of heaven and earth, from whom Jesus came, whose mission He is carrying out, and to whom He will return. In verse 33 the aorist subjunctive (*arnēsētai me*) looks back on the past life of the denier, while *an* adds a vividness that heightens the expectancy that such deniers will be found. The accusative *me* emphasizes a complete breach with Christ. The person is saying no to Christ.

"Confess" here means to make a statement or to bear witness. In the last judgment, confession or denial will be rewarded by Christ as the Judge of the world, according to Luke 12:8. Here and now it will be confirmed and disclosed to the Father by Christ. Importance is attached to the correspondence between human conduct on earth and the eschatological word of the Judge or Witness. The Christian's confession here on earth is therefore of definitive importance.

The term *martureō* (bear witness) is to be distinguished from *homologeō.*

> All *marturein* is a *homologein,* but not vice versa. The point of *marturein* is that believers should be won. In *homologein* there is a firm declaration of what is in a man, but with no necessary effect on those around. The opposite of *homologein* is *arneisthai,* that of *marturein diōkein.* The Pharisees confess angels and the resurrection (Acts 23:8), but they do not bear witness to them. Sins are confessed, but one does not testify to them. One can, of course, 'witness' a confession (1 Tim. 6:13). The task of the witness in the early Christian sense is to make known a specific fact or truth. In *homologein* one stands personally behind something which one thinks, or believes, or has done, before a judge (Acts 24:14), or men (Rom. 10:9–10), or persecutors (Matt. 10:32), or the congregation (1 Tim. 6:12). (Gerhard Kittel, ed., *Theological Dictionary of the New Testament* [Grand Rapids, Mich.: Wm. B. Eerdmans Publishing Co., 1967], 4:497)

"Confess" also implies a previous relationship of obedience and faithfulness. It can take place only where there has first been acknowledgment and commitment. Someone who denies the person of Jesus Christ has failed to meet the claim of Jesus Christ for a confession of discipleship. The recorded instance of this is Peter's denial. The same possibility often arose with the martyrs. Anxiety that the world will regard one with contempt can also be a denial of Christ. Being ashamed of the Lord and trying to get honor from the world brings the Lord into contempt. Peter, of course, denied Jesus because of fear. Similarly, during the times of persecution many denied and sacrificed to idols or to Caesar because they feared the threats of those in power. In other cases there was fear of losing human favor and the advantages that other people could offer.

Furthermore, to deny Christ is not to be at His disposal to meet the needs of one's neighbors. Thus any unethical conduct may be described as a denial of Christ. Finally, a person who fails to acknowledge Christ in sound doctrine also denies Him. When statements about Christ have consequences for practical decisions of life, they need to be made correctly and cautiously. There is not only the inner connection between teaching and practice to be considered but also the fact that any false statement about Christ denies Him. Christ's claim extends even to one's thinking.

Jesus promises His disciples that He will confess them before the divine Judge and thus assure them against condemnation. The last judgment will therefore mean their deliverance, and they can look forward to it even though their discipleship entails persecutions. On the other hand, those who deny Him will be overwhelmed by eternal misery. The relation to Jesus is therefore decisive. Jesus sets forth the judgment of God as a reality of the conscience, as something that is unconditionally accepted by those aware of moral responsibility. The word of Jesus finally decides human destiny.

Stated and Suggested Truths of the Text

The whole Christian life, in outward word and deed and inward thought and motive, is to be ordered by obedience to Christ. The whole person must evince the confession of the heart that Christ is Savior and Lord. Such persons Jesus will confess before the Father. Those who deny Him with their lives Jesus will deny before the Father. They may talk about Him and even give a display of religion, but Christ, who knows their hearts, knows they are not His.

We confess Christ when we speak to others of what Christ and His Word mean to us and when we share Christ and His Word in ordinary situations in ways that are natural for us. But words must be supported with actions. Jesus reminds us that "not everyone who says to me, 'Lord, Lord,' will enter the kingdom of heaven, but only he who does the will of my Father who is in heaven" (Matt. 7:21). The challenge is to live like Christ's people. "Let your light shine before men, that they may see your good deeds and praise your Father in heaven" (Matt. 5:16). Our good deeds prove the sincerity of our faith as we let our faith in Christ affect everything we do. To confess Christ means to be a little Christ in word and deed and prayer.

There is a unity in the diversity of ways Christ has been confessed in many languages and in many places, in all generations and among all peoples. That unity is based on what God through Jesus Christ has done to and for the world as witnessed by the Old and New Testament Scriptures.

We cannot confess Jesus Christ before the world without at the same time asking God's forgiveness for our own sin and being grateful for having experienced God's goodness and mercy. Confession of sin, praise of Christ, and witness to His Gospel in word and deed before the world belong together inseparably. Where one of these is missing, the confession is falsified.

We not only believe in the existence of truth, but we place our trust in the truth—the truth of Jesus who has saved us and who can be confessed in the world. But if the world is to take us seriously, we must practice the truth. Otherwise tough-minded youngsters who go off to universities and are taught that all is relative in the fields of sociology, psychology, and philosophy will not take us seriously. Practicing the truth is a matter of loyalty to Jesus Christ.

Our confession of Christ becomes crucially important in a world where many people think that those of different faiths are in different boats but all heading for the same shore; that it doesn't make any difference what people believe as long as they are sincere; that what makes a person a Christian is believing in the Golden Rule and the Ten Commandments.

In the Bible, mysteries are not explained; they are proclaimed. So it is, for example, with the virgin birth of Christ, His miracles, and His resurrection. Our primary task as confessors is not to explain but to proclaim. The message of Christ's death and resurrection has power to remove obstacles that prevent people from believing. Jesus Christ is Himself the truth; in His light, falsehood is exposed.

Parallel Passages—Confession

. . . and every tongue confess that Jesus Christ is Lord to the glory of God the Father (Phil. 2:11). He did not fail to confess, but confessed freely, "I am not the Christ" (John 1:20). Yet at the same time many even among the leaders believed in him. But because of the Pharisees they would not confess their faith for fear they would be put out of the synagogue; for they loved praise from men more than praise from God (John 12:42–43). If you confess with your mouth, "Jesus is Lord," and believe in your heart that God raised him from the dead, you will be saved. For it is with your heart that you believe and are justified, and it is with your mouth that you confess and are saved (Rom. 10:9–10). Whoever acknowledges the Son has the Father also (1 John 2:23). Every spirit that acknowledges that Jesus Christ has come in the flesh is from God, but every spirit that does not acknowledge Jesus is not from God (1 John 4:2–3). If anyone acknowledges that Jesus is the Son of God, God lives in him and he in God (1 John 4:15). I . . . will acknowledge his name before my Father and his angels (Rev. 3:5). Beyond all question, the mystery of godliness is great: He appeared in a body, was vindicated by the Spirit, was seen by angels, was preached among the nations, was believed on in the world, was taken up in glory (1 Tim. 3:16). Take hold of the eternal life to which you were called when you made your good confession in the presence of many witnesses. In the sight of God, who gives life to everything, and of Christ Jesus, who while testifying before Pontius Pilate made the good confession (1 Tim. 6:12–13). Let us hold firmly to the faith we profess (Heb. 4:14). Let us hold unswervingly to the hope we profess, for he who promised is faithful (Heb. 10:23). He must deny himself and take up his cross and follow me (Matt. 16:24). Even if I have to die with you, I will never disown you (Matt. 26:35). He denied it again, with an oath (Matt. 26:72). You disowned the Holy and Righteous One (Acts 3:14). If we disown him, he will also disown us (2 Tim. 2:12). They claim to know God, but by their actions they deny him. They are detestable, disobedient and unfit for doing anything good (Titus 1:16). No one who denies the Son has the Father (1 John 2:23). You have kept my word and have not denied my name (Rev. 3:8). Always be prepared to give an answer to everyone who asks you to give the reason for the hope that you have. But do this with gentleness and respect, keeping a clear conscience, so that those who speak maliciously against your good behavior in Christ may be ashamed of their slander (1 Peter 3:15–16).

The Central Thought

Both the confession and the denial of Christ before people have divine and eternal consequences.

Goal

The goal of the sermon is that the hearers publicly profess their commitment to Christ. The problem is that fear of what others may think of us or do to us often causes us to hide our relationship to Christ. The means to the goal is that Christ, by delivering us from the final judgment, has freed us from the fear of human judgment.

Sermon Outline

Introduction: You are on a camping trip with some of your friends. One evening after supper, as you are sitting outside the tent, the conversation turns to religion, and someone says, "It doesn't matter what a person believes as long as he is sincere." Others voice their agreement. What will you say?

Maybe you are a housewife getting acquainted with your next-door neighbor, a woman about your age with three young children. In the course of the conversation she says to you, "We don't send our children to Sunday school or church. We don't think it's right to force religion on them. They can choose whatever religion they like when they're old enough and wise enough to make their own choice." What will you say?

If you're a young person, your friends may say to you, "Anybody who wants to get ahead in this world has got to look out for himself; he has got to do what is best for good old Number One." What would you say?

Have we been concerned that others will think us odd and that we will lose out on certain advantages if we witness to our commitment to Christ? Peter was so afraid of what others might do to him that he even denied that he ever knew Christ.

Jesus points out that failure to witness to Him has serious consequences. But He also gives us positive encouragement to witness. Tonight we will consider

Outline :   **Lent: A Time for Renewal of Witness**

I. There is more than one way to witness to Christ.
   A. We witness to Jesus Christ when we make clear that a person's relationship to Him is of decisive importance.
      1. Whether we are responding to statements like those of the campers, the woman next door, or the young people or answering a question someone has put to us about our religious beliefs (1 Peter 3:15), we need to point to Christ as the only Savior.
      2. We talk about Christ's dying for us on the cross so that our sins are forgiven and God no longer condemns us.
      3. We talk about how important it is to believe in Jesus Christ. Only in Christ can anyone be acceptable to God and have eternal life (Acts 4:12).
   B. We witness to Christ when we confess our faith in Him in the word of the liturgy, the Creed, the catechism, and other confessional writings of our church (Heb. 10:23).
      1. In our country we don't have to be afraid of confessing Christ in a worship service, but in some countries it takes considerable courage to do so.
      2. We may be afraid to confess Christ by contending for sound doctrine because others might regard us as obscurantists or Biblicists.
      3. Yet loyalty to Christ cannot be separated from loyalty to His Word.
   C. We witness to Christ when we live in a way that honors Him.
      1. Deeds that conform to God's moral standard, not the world's, bring honor to Christ (Matt. 5:16).
      2. We act lovingly toward others, valuing them because of their dignity rather than their utility. This dignity rests on the fact that we all have been dearly purchased by the blood of Christ.
      3. We renounce not merely our sins but ourselves and allow ourselves to be established by Christ and conformed more and more to His image.

We can be less fearful and inhibited about witnessing when we remember that there is more than one way to witness to Christ before people. What matters is that Christ is exalted and that we are ready to back our witness. But more than knowledge of how to witness is needed if we are going to be renewed in our witness.

II. There is only one way to be renewed in our witness to Christ.
   A. We look to Christ as our defender before God.
      1. When Jesus comes at the end of time to judge, He will acknowledge us who have confessed Him. We have nothing to fear on the last great day. So we have nothing to fear now.
      2. On the other hand, that Christ will also be the accuser at the

judgment of those who have denied Him tells us that there will be those who once confessed Christ but who, for fear of losing the favor of people, finally said no to Christ. If we are to avoid such a fate, we must repent of any denial of Christ by word or deed.

3. If we have been unfaithful at times in our witnessing, He remains faithful and will not deny Himself (2 Tim. 2:11). He will not go back on His promise to forgive us and to confess before His Father all who by faith have endeavored to confess Him.

B. We rely on His Gospel to remove our fear and renew our witness.

1. The Gospel message of Christ's death and resurrection can empower us because it does not tell us that we must witness to merit Christ's approval. Christ acknowledges us by sheer grace and regards our witness highly.

2. Our primary task is to proclaim the Gospel, not to explain or defend it. The Gospel itself has the power to remove obstacles that prevent people from believing.

Conclusion: It is time for renewal of our witness. We have something of crucial importance to say. Whichever way we say it, Christ will defend and strengthen us.

Sermon Illustrations

Several students were walking across the quadrangle of a large university just as the bell tower chimed five o'clock in the afternoon. At that precise moment in front of them on the sidewalk a foreign student dropped full length on the ground to the utter amazement of those walking behind him. After the initial shock the students realized that he had not stumbled or fallen but was a Moslem who was prostrating himself at his holy hour of prayer.

That man was not ashamed of his religion. How many of us are not ashamed to make known that we are Christians ... ?

How many of us by omission of prayer, or other practices that might designate that we are Christians, in effect become guilty of the sin of the apostle Peter when he said: "I do not know the Man" (Matthew 26:74)?

What a tragedy for those who have been nominal members of the church, but about whom Christ will one day say: "And then will I declare to them, 'I never knew you' "! (Matthew 7:23).

Donald Deffner, *Bold Ones on Campus* (CPH, 1973), p. 63.

The one agnostic was puzzled as he said to his fellow doubter, "Why do you go to hear that fellow preach all the time? You don't believe the stuff that he says, do you?"

"No," said his friend in reply, "but he does."

The preacher they were referring to was unashamed of preaching the Gospel of Jesus Christ. Yet it was not a Gospel of his own making, nor did he have a power from within himself that caused the one doubter to come back again and again to hear what he had to say. We recall the example in the Book of Acts when two of our Lord's disciples were fulfilling the missionary calling with which the Lord had entrusted them, and the Scripture says: "Now when they saw the boldness of Peter and John and perceived that they were uneducated, common men, they wondered; and they recognized that they had been with Jesus" (Acts 4:13).

Deffner, *Bold Ones*, p. 150.

Somewhere I once read about pilgrims who visit certain temples in Jerusalem. The incense is heavy. And as the pilgrims return to their homes or accost friends on the street, the others can tell where they have been.

Can others tell where *you* have been, where you are coming from, and where you are going?

Have your eyes "seen the King"?

Somebody once said that "the far country" in the story of the Prodigal Son is *any condition in your life*—wherever you are—which keeps you away from God.

What "land" are you in right now?

Donald Deffner, *The Possible Years* (CPH, 1973), p. 55.

A college student was chatting with a friend of his about his coming job in the north woods. His friend said: "I wonder if you really know what you're letting yourself in for. That's a pretty rough lot of men up there."

When the summer had passed, the two friends met again. The one asked the other: "Well, how did you, *a Christian,* make out with that crowd?"

"Oh," said the other, "I didn't really have any trouble. *They never caught on!*"

Deffner, *The Possible Years*, p. 56.

Indirect advertising is indeed important and often more effective than the direct pitch. So is the indirect witness for Christ. The believer who reveals Christ by the way he lives, moves, walks, talks, eats, reads, pays his bills, . . . will probably do more than the fanatic with the sandwich board that reads: "Prepare to meet thy God."

Donald Grey Barnhouse, *Let Me Illustrate* (Revell, 1976), p. 348.

Dr. Howard Kelly, famed surgeon of Baltimore and renowned for the Christian principles he maintained in his profession, was seldom seen without a beautiful rosebud in the lapel of his coat. It remained fresh for a long time—and there was a reason. When people asked him the secret, he turned the lapel and showed them a little glass vial containing water. The stem of the rose went through the buttonhole into the water and thus kept fresh for a longer time. Dr. Kelly would then tell inquirers that the secret of beautiful and fragrant Christian living lies in drawing refreshment from the water of life, Jesus Christ.

Wilbur E. Nelson, *Anecdotes and Illustrations* (Baker, 1971), p. 44.

"Aunt Sophie," a converted scrubwoman who said she was "called to scrub and preach" was made fun of by someone who said she was seen talking about Christ even to a wooden Indian in front of a cigar store. Sophie replied: "Perhaps I did. My eyesight is not so good. But talking to a wooden Indian about Christ is not so bad as being a wooden Christian and never talking to anybody about the Lord Jesus.

Nelson, p. 45.

Joni Erickson is a quadriplegic who draws pictures with a pen in her teeth. For eight years she has been immovable from her shoulders down after suffering a broken neck from a dive into shallow waters of Chesapeake Bay. Though she had become a Christian in high school through the witness of her friends in the local Young Life group, after her accident she became bitter, feeling there was no reason for living. But God saw her through those extremely difficult times and she finally decided that God must care. Through prayer and Bible study, she returned to faith in God and her life is on an upward swing. Joni has now completed more than 250 drawings, has a line of greeting cards, and accepts orders for originals. In an appearance on TV's "Today Show," she shared her faith and conviction that God has a reason for her being in a wheelchair saying, "I want Him to be glorified through me." ... She writes "P.T.L." under her signature on each drawing and tells those who are curious that it means "Praise the Lord." "And then I tell them why I want to praise Him. He is what life is all about."

A. Dudley Dennison Jr., *Windows, Ladders and Bridges* (Zondervan, 1976), p. 152.

As she reflected upon the Miss America Pageant, Vonda Kay Van Dyke commented, "I was a Christian competing in a contest that some 'religious' people would criticize me for entering." ... She smiled as she recalled the tense moments that preceded her title selection. "I was sitting up there in the top five. I paused and prayed that something come up in questioning that would allow me to share my Christian faith with the millions watching television." Then came Bert Parks's challenging query: "I understand that you always carry a Bible with you. Do you consider your Bible a good-luck charm?" "I do not consider my Bible a good-luck charm; it is the most important book I own. My relationship to God is not a religion but a faith. I believe in Him, trust in Him and pray that even tonight His will might be done." "I couldn't have asked for a better question!" she said later. "I prayed the Lord would help me in answering the question, and He definitely did."

John McDowell in *Evidence That Demands a Verdict,* quoted by Dennison, p. 208.

I've got to admit that I spend a LOT more time seeking business successes than I do seeking success as a Christian. I can go nine to five, Monday through Friday, without giving God a thought. I NEVER do that to business—not even when I'm on vacation!

As a world at large, we're pretty swept up in business and our occupation. We have gotten carried away with the IMPORTANCE of what we do for a living and how successful we have become at it.

Wally Armbruster, *It's Still Lion vs. Christian in the Corporate Arena* (CPH, 1979), p. 25.

It becomes a decision of who we will sacrifice to . . . the organization god or the Other One.

I've heard the Organization Man described as "that frightening symbol of elastic ethics and compromise." I could describe him as a . . . Christian who is more afraid of losing his job or his place on the Corporate Ladder than he is of losing his soul. But I'm not insensitive to his dilemma. It ain't easy.

Armbruster, p. 29.

We can be motivated by ideals, by idylls, or by idols. . . .

When business pursuits stop being just something you'd like to have and start becoming something you NEED, you're not far from getting on your knees . . . not far from bowing to business considerations even if they conflict with God considerations.

Armbruster, pp. 34–35.

It's dangerous for a Christian to set even heaven as his bottom-line goal. He ought to seek loving and serving God and shining the Light before others.

Heaven, too (I think) could become a god—more highly prized than God Himself.

Armbruster, p. 41.

Try mentioning God in the middle of a business discussion and watch what funny looks you get. Try saying, "I disapprove of marketing this new product because it appeals to people's prurient interests and is therefore unchristian" or "We shouldn't have this Christmas sale because it exploits a holy occasion" or "We shouldn't bury this as a business expense because that would be a sin." You can guess how far you will get.

Armbruster, p. 28.

JESUS, I need You to remind me that even though I'm part of management, I still belong to a union: the brotherhood of Christ. To which I must pay my dues. I need You to remind me that competitors, fellow employees, suppliers, and customers are people You love as much as You love me and that I am supposed to do likewise. Show me (for I am blind) the many opportunities I have each day to let people see You through me....

LORD, I also thank You. I thank you for granting me whatever talent I have for the business I'm in ... and for enjoying my work. Remind me to treat it as sacred, as a vocation, as a means to fulfill my Christian commitment ... not as a separate island of my life. Most of all Lord, remind me that I *am* baptized ... not "was" baptized ... every minute of every day, especially from nine to five.

Armbruster, p. 117.

Lent: A Time for Renewal of True Religion

They tie up heavy loads and put them on men's shoulders,
but they themselves are not willing to lift a finger to move
them. (Matt. 23:4)

Matthew 26:57–68; John 11:45–53

Introduction

It is interesting to note that in much of contemporary literature and in the media "preacher" and "phony" are often used almost synonymously. This says something about the animosity that the world has toward ministers of the Gospel, but it also says something about the phoniness that is often perceived in the church and its spokesmen. This is a subject about which the preacher needs to take time for real self-examination. It's just about impossible for a preacher who is perceived by many of his members to be a phony to deliver an effective sermon on true religion.

Nobody likes a phony. Perhaps we are better at spotting phoniness in others than in ourselves. Phonies are people who make sure that their names are on the letterhead of civic and charitable work. Phonies take courses in listening skills and sensitivity training, but they use their training to manipulate people rather than to help. The insincerity of phonies is eventually spotted. They use people. They are pretenders.

The worst phonies are phony Christians, for false and hypocritical Christians can hurt the faith of others and eventually come to believe their own lies. Phony religion led to the excesses of the Crusades in the Middle Ages and to the Spanish Inquisition. Phony religion made the Reformation necessary. It is phony religion that is preached and proclaimed so often by some radio and television preachers.

The worst thing that can be said about phony religion is that it operates with the premise that the end justifies the means. Religious fanatics believe that they alone have the truth and that everyone else is the enemy. The enemy is evil, so the enemy must be defeated. The means toward that end can be anything, for truth justifies any excess. Thus, in the name of religion, bombs explode in Belfast and Beirut.

The Passion account focuses on Jesus and His confrontation with Caiaphas. Jesus represents true religion; Caiaphas represents false religion that has gotten out of hand. Caiaphas lived with the premise that the end justifies the means.

The Way of Phony Religion

Caiaphas, the high priest, was surely a product of his times. Israel had not taken God seriously for much of its history. False religion crept in, and Israel

became more secular than religious. The religion that did exist was insti-
tutionalized. The Pharisees were a lay movement that began as a reaction
to Israel's religious casualness, but there was nothing casual about the Pharisees. They especially took to heart the 613 rules that interpreted the commands of God, and they kept those rules, insisting that others do the same.
For them religion was not a matter of the heart responding to God's love.
It was a matter of keeping rules and regulations. Those rules left no room
for the weak, yet penitent, believer.

Caiaphas operated out of that background. He was the high priest, a
position he shared with Annas. He held the highest position within the
religious establishment. Jesus had just raised Lazarus from the dead, and this
was reported to the Pharisees. They requested a meeting of the council of
70—called the Sanhedrin, the highest ecclesiastical court—to consider what
Jesus had done. They could explain away an unsubstantiated miracle in the
back country of Galilee but not this. It had happened in a suburb, Bethany,
and it wasn't simply a miracle worker giving sight to the blind and hearing
to the deaf. Jesus had raised Lazarus from the dead, *publicly* bringing to
life a man who had been entombed for four days. Lazarus was living proof
that Jesus was more than a mere miracle worker. The authorities knew what
they had to deal with—at least Caiaphas knew. They had the Messiah to
deal with, and this Messiah had openly and persistently criticized their
phoniness. Remember what Jesus said? Read Matthew 23:13–36.

Of all people, Caiaphas should have known better. Despite his wickedness,
the Holy Spirit still worked in him. He and the 70 should have rejoiced and
said: "Finally! The Messiah has come! And since He is the Messiah, we had
better listen and repent and be renewed. Let's find Him and worship Him!"

This isn't what happened, as we know. The leaders feared for their positions. They were afraid of losing their privileged arrangement with Rome.
They had reached an accommodation with the Roman authorities, who in
effect said: "Keep things quiet and under control, and you can practice your
religion. Let things get out of hand, and we'll crush any revolt, disperse the
people, destroy your temple, and your religion will disappear." It is note-
worthy that not one word was said in the Sanhedrin about the spirit of the
Old Testament prophets. There were no courageous statements of "as for
me and my house ...," no trusting expressions of "the Lord is my Shepherd. ..." A decision was made. Jesus' miracles must not be allowed to go
on.

After the discussion had proceeded for a time, Caiaphas impatiently took
charge. "You know nothing at all! You do not realize that it is better ..."
The end justifies the means. Jesus must die for the sake of the people. John
adds the crucial words: "He did not say this on his own, but as high priest
that year he prophesied that Jesus would die for the Jewish nation, and not
only for that nation but also for the scattered children of God, to bring them
together and make them one" (John 11:51–52).

John further states: "So from that day on they plotted to take his life" (v.
53). The end justified the means, even if others must die for the sake of

their privileged positions. That's the way phony religion works. John adds further: "Meanwhile a large crowd of Jews found out that Jesus was there and came, not only because of him but also to see Lazarus, whom he had raised from the dead. So the chief priests made plans to kill Lazarus as well, for on account of him many of the Jews were going over to Jesus and putting their faith in him" (12:9–11).

The end justifies the means. So they sought to arrest Jesus, put Him on trial, and dispose of Him quietly and secretly. Judas furthered their plans, and Jesus was arrested in the Garden of Gethsemane. False witnesses were brought forward to make accusations against Jesus, but their testimony didn't agree. (At least two witnesses had to agree before charges could be brought.) Then Caiaphas took charge of a situation that was getting out of hand and put Jesus under oath. When Jesus responded to his question, Caiaphas, overdramatizing the situation, tore his robes and cried, "Blasphemy!" There was no examination at this trial of who Jesus truly was. There was no real conversation. There was no listening and praying, no seeking and hoping. This is false religion at its worst. And the judgment? "Guilty!" Now they would need to convince Pilate that a purely religious crime was also a civil crime against Rome, that this Jesus was a threat that had to be removed.

Spotting Phony Religion

One of the readings in the liturgy designed for the fourth Lenten service is from Galatians. It concerns a phony gospel that had been brought to the Galatians and would, the apostle Paul knew, inevitably lead to the destruction of the true Gospel. Another reading deals with the phoniness of some Corinthian Christians that led to exclusivity and coldness. The first of the three readings speaks more directly to our point. "They tie up heavy loads and put them on men's shoulders, but they themselves are not willing to lift a finger to move them" (Matt. 23:4). Two books come to mind. One is *Religion Can Be Hazardous to Your Health,* and the other is *How to Be Christian without Being Religious.* In both instances "religion" is a bad word. The scribes, Pharisees, and Caiaphas were all religious. It was their religion that got into the way of true faith. The best summary of what had happened in the hearts of the Pharisees is found in Luke 15:2: "The Pharisees and the teachers of the law muttered, 'This man welcomes sinners and eats with them.' " Jesus wasn't religious! He received people who didn't keep the 613 rules! He ate dinner with them! Jesus wasn't good!

Phony religion happens when "goodness" becomes the central mark of the Christian life. Those who are "good" are considered believers. Those who are not "good" are not believers. In this view, the church is composed only of "good" people. No one else may apply. When goodness is the mark, one of two things happens. We either become phonies and hypocrites, or we are led to despair. That is, if we must be good, we will try to keep whatever rules need to be kept in order to be considered good. Inevitably, we will eventually either get tired of living rigidly under the rules (many children do and rebel), or we will cover up every bad thing we do. If goodness is the rule, we will have absolutely no word of hope for those who don't keep the rules, for there is no hope. On the other hand, we may not try to cover them up, but the result will be just as tragic; we will have nowhere to go. If only good people can be accepted by a good God and His good followers, we can despair of any hope. This is precisely why Jesus said: "Woe to you, teachers of the law and Pharisees, you hypocrites! You shut the kingdom of heaven in men's faces. You yourselves do not enter, nor will you let those enter who are trying to. Woe to you, teachers of the law and Pharisees, you hypocrites! You travel over land and sea to win a single convert, and when he becomes one, you make him twice as much a son of hell as you are" (Matt. 23:13–15).

Breaking Through toward True Religion

Jesus broke through the goodness trap and insisted that the mark of the believer is not *goodness*. It is *forgiveness*. While the Pharisees and scribes grumbled and whispered, "This man receives sinners," the sinners *rejoiced* to say, "This man receives sinners and eats with them!" The lost sheep is the person who knows that he or she has strayed, has not been good, and is lost forever *except that* the Good Shepherd goes to the bramble bush of the cross, takes our badness on Himself, and dies. But out of an open tomb He comes, shouting for all to hear, "Look who I found! Rejoice with me!" The Shepherd is carrying you and me!

The renewal of true religion happens when we confess that our religion of goodness is false. It gets in the way of the Good Shepherd. True religion happens when we know and believe that we lost sheep have been found; that is what the Christian faith is all about. We have a Savior who receives sinners and communes with them, lives in them, changes their hearts into hearts of love, and enables them to say with gladness and joy: "There's hope for others, for look at what God has done and is still doing for someone like me!"

The challenge for the preacher is to be able to identify areas where phony religion must be overcome by the true religion that comes from the cross. We suggest a few: True religion happens when we make sure that our lives say: "Jesus receives sinners and eats with them. Look at me. I'm not good; I am forgiven!" We need to say this to those who have wronged us, so that they may know another way to live. We need to say this to our own children, so that they are not burdened with guilt for not being good but are filled with the joy of being forgiven sinners like their parents. We need to say this in our churches, so that none fail to enter our churches because they feel unworthy or leave without knowing that Jesus invites them, receives them, and forgives them.

Goodness is not wrong, of course. We ought to be good, for goodness is a fruit of the Spirit and a means of service to our neighbor. But goodness is not our chief mark as Christians. Faith in Jesus Christ, who forgives our lack of goodness, is our chief mark. Caiaphas declared Jesus to be "not good—guilty." Yet that was God's plan. The innocent Jesus, good in every way, was declared guilty so that He might take our guilt on Himself to the cross and crucify that guilt to death in His body. So we live by faith in Christ, our substitute and the source of goodness.

Faith is not static. It is not a set of religious propositions behind which we can conveniently hide. Faith is a relationship that trusts in God's mercy and responds in godly actions. To proclaim that Christian education is important without growing in it and making sure that our Sunday school children grow in it is phony. To say that we have an important mission and ministry as Christ's church without supporting it with our time, talent, and treasure is phony. To say that Christ has called us to demonstrate our faith through acts of loving service to the world around us without acting on that belief is phony. It is to be "religious" without true religion. Yet in confessing our phoniness, we see Jesus, our Good Shepherd, standing before us, wanting to put His nail-marked hands into the bramble bush where we have strayed.

Sermon Outline

Introduction: The Lenten renewal subject placed before us today will make all of us squirm a little—or perhaps a great deal! The opposite of true religion is false religion, and who among us isn't guilty of a little playacting about our religion, especially in the way we live it? Who among us doesn't have a public face and a private face, a spiritual "sitting room" where we entertain company and a spiritual "family room" where the real person sits—warts and all!

Nobody likes a phony. But the worst phony is the religious phony. In the worst religious phony we can imagine, Caiaphas, we see the confrontation between phony religion and true religion, who is Jesus. In the meeting of these two, we are confronted with

Outline :   Lent: A Time for Renewal of True Religion
  I. How phony religion happens: Caiaphas
     A. A product of his time
     B. The event that could not be ignored
     C. What Caiaphas should have known and acknowledged
     D. Fear produced phoniness
     E. The end justifies the means
 II. How to spot phony religion
     A. Heavy burdens are laid on people
     B. Religion becomes a bad word
     C. Goodness becomes religion's chief mark
III. How to break through to true religion
     A. Jesus breaks through the phoniness by seeking the "not good"
     B. Jesus causes renewal to happen
     C. Learn what it looks like
     D. Seek true religion!

Conclusion: What a terrible thing phony religion is! It is essentially living a lie, not just before people but before God. That was the tragedy of Caiaphas. That's the tragedy that can befall us if we live the lie that we are good, for then we don't need God. But we do need Him, for we are not good. God knows that. He gave us Jesus. Regardless of the bramble bush of guilt, of self-protection, or of a judgmental nature in which you live, let go with a shout: "Here I am, hiding, guilty, helpless. Reach for me, God!" He will! He has—in Jesus. And He will put you on His shoulder rejoicing, and you also will rejoice!

Lent: A Time for Renewal of Priorities

Do not love the world or anything in the world. If anyone loves the world, the love of the Father is not in him. For everything in the world—the cravings of sinful man, the lust of his eyes and the boasting of what he has and does— comes not from the Father but from the world. The world and its desires pass away, but the man who does the will of God lives forever. (1 John 2:15–17)

John 18:28–19:16

The Text in Its Context

How does the text relate to the life of the author and the situation of those he addresses?

The first letter of John, written while John was exercising his ministry at Ephesus, was occasioned by two false teachings threatening the churches in the surrounding country: the antinomianism of the Nicolaitans and the Gnosticism of Cerinthus. The Nicolaitans taught that even a person living in sin might still be spiritual and a child of God, while the Gnostics denied that Christ is truly God and truly man, human and divine. Yet John's purpose in writing is not only polemical. He inculcates love for God manifested by love for the brotherhood and inspired by the love God first showed us. John had not always been the apostle of love. He had been self-seeking (Mark 10:35–45) and fiery, meriting the title "Son of Thunder" (3:17). John also wishes to assure his readers that when they believe in the love that God has for them in Christ, they have eternal life. "I write these things to you who believe in the name of the Son of God so that you may know that you have eternal life" (1 John 5:13).

How does the text fit the general purpose and outline of the book?

The false teachers John has in mind had turned the grace of God into lasciviousness and had also denied a fundamental truth about the person of Jesus Christ. John calls these teachers "antichrists" because they are truly hostile to Christianity. They are not of God but are of the world. Therefore, to love the world in such a way as to live in the lusts of the flesh associated with the unbelieving world is to exclude oneself from fellowship with God and with the children of God. The child of God is not to give first priority to an evil world that is destined to pass away.

John sets forth profound truths in brief phrases, emphasized by rhythmic and poetic repetitions. Although the unity of the epistle is apparent, the structure is more spiral than linear. Generally speaking, 1:5–2:29 discusses the life of fellowship with God that is demonstrated by love for fellow believers and refusal to love the world (2:7–17).

What light does the material immediately before and after the text throw on the text itself?

It is clear from 2:12–14 that John is writing to Christians to encourage their progress and to caution them against temptations. In verse 12 the term "dear children" applies to all the readers to whom John stands in the affectionate relation of a spiritual father. In verse 13 he addresses the more mature Christians and also the younger Christians. He is writing to them because their sins are forgiven (v. 12), they know the Father (v. 13), and they have overcome the evil one (v. 14). An additional reason for writing to the more mature Christians is that they know Christ, who is from the beginning. Readers who know the Father are ready to heed the warning "Love not the world." Those who know the eternal Christ are prepared to resist seduction by things that eventually pass away. Those who have overcome the evil one are ready to resist attacks of sinful cravings, the lust of the eyes, and prideful boasting.

In verse 18 John again addresses all his readers as "dear children." Having reminded them of the impermanence of the world, he can also affirm that they are living in the closing or last hour, in the time preceding Christ's final return. John does not pretend to know the precise time of Christ's return, but the appearance of such antichrists as Cerinthus and his followers is a sure sign that the last period of the world's history has begun.

How does this text relate to the person and work of Jesus Christ, to the milieu of the early church, and to the Old Testament background?

John is writing to Christians who have experienced the grace of Christ and whom he can therefore urge to remain faithful to Christ. It would be useless to warn those still of the world not to love the world. Because his readers know the Father and the Son, have forgiveness of sins, and have overcome the evil one, John can urge them not to love the evil world. Christians are not immune to the enticements, allurements, and blandishments of the world. Love of the world had often proved to be the undoing of the people of God in the Old Testament. The Israelites became attached to the false gods, false worship, and evil practices of the heathen people surrounding them. From the beginning God's people have needed to prioritize their values and activities.

The Textual Study

A. In the original

There is no significant variation of the text in the apparatus.

The present imperative *agapate* (v. 15) forbids deliberate and continuous loving of the world. For Christians it is a matter of the will; they can choose whether or not to love the world.

The "world" (*kosmon*) in verse 15 does not refer to the world of nature with its changing seasons, sunlight, flowers, mountains, and seas, or to the world of human relationships with its duties, joys, friendships, struggles, triumphs, and tears. The reference is to the world of unbelieving men and women and to all the immoral tendencies and pursuits that give the world an evil character. We are not to love this world in the sense of courting its favors, following its customs, adopting its maxims, or coveting its prizes. We have the right to admire, appreciate, and properly use all the world's physical objects and natural beauties, but whatever in the world is hostile to God and to Christ and His kingdom, no matter how alluring or attractive it appears, we must oppose. The heart set on the evil world cannot at the same time be filled with love for the Father.

In verse 16 John mentions some of these sinful things: *epithumia tēs sarkos* is sinful desire springing from the depraved nature, the gratification of which enslaves the soul; *epithumia tōn ophthalmōn* refers to lust that reaches beyond what a person can actually get hold of in sinning, the appeal being to the eyes and thus to the mind and the imagination. In this connection we need to be alert to the world's attempt to cover its vileness with aesthetic appeals. Finally, there is *alazoneia*, the vain glory of life, the pride of place and possessions expressing itself in a foolish sense of security and a satisfaction in things that will soon vanish. The reference is also to pretentiousness and ostentation for the purpose of outshining our neighbors. *Bios* here refers to the life peculiar to human beings in contrast to *zōē*, the life principle that humanity shares with God.

The three forms of evil referred to above can be dangerous at different periods of a person's life, but they form the familiar features of "the world."

They do not come out of the Father but out of the world, the preposition *ek* expressing source. The Father is the source of life and blessing; the world is the source of lust and death. That is why love of the Father and love of the world are absolutely incompatible.

In verse 17 John gives yet another reason that we are not to love the world. The world is passing away (*paragetai*); its decay has begun, its doom is overtaking it. Even if it were not passing away, human capacity for enjoying it must certainly come to an end, as the sensualist finds out. So to love the world is to lose everything, including the thing loved, but to love God is to gain Him and His kingdom. The world is waning; God and God alone and His believers abide. To be doing the will of God includes believing in His Son and living the life of obedience that follows from belief. Such a person, in contrast to the passing world, abides forever.

B. In the vernacular
How do the translations help me understand possible idiomatic expressions in the text? The paraphrase by Phillips expresses the meaning in a fresh way:

> *Never give your hearts to this world or to*
> *any of the things in it. A man cannot love*
> *the Father and love the world at the same*
> *time. For the world system, based as it is on*
> *men's primitive desires, their greedy ambi-*

> *tions, and the glamour of all that they think*
> *splendid, is not derived from the Father at*
> *all, but from the world itself. The world and*
> *all its passionate desires will one day disap-*
> *pear. But the man who is following God's*
> *will is part of the permanent and cannot*
> *die.*

The NEB in its typically direct way conveys other nuances:

> *Do not set your hearts on the godless world*
> *or anything in it. Anyone who loves the*
> *world is a stranger to the Father's love. Ev-*
> *erything the world affords, all that panders*
> *to the appetites or entices the eyes, all the*
> *glamour of its life, springs not from the Fa-*
> *ther but from the godless world. And that*
> *world is passing away with all its allure-*
> *ments, but he who does God's will stands*
> *forevermore.*

Closest to the original is the NASB:

> *All that is in the world, the lust of the flesh*
> *and the lust of the eyes and the boastful*
> *pride of life, is not from the Father, but is*
> *from the world. And the world is passing*
> *away and also its lusts; but the one who*
> *does the will of God abides forever.*

At the end of verse 17 TEV has: "but he who does what God wants lives forever." TEV has the following for verse 16:

> *Everything that belongs to the world—what*
> *the sinful self desires, what people see and*
> *want, and everything in this world that peo-*
> *ple are so proud of—none of this is from the*
> *Father; it all comes from the world.*

The NIV translates verse 16:

> *For everything in the world—the cravings of*
> *sinful man, the lust of his eyes and his pride*
> *in possessions. . . ."*

In verse 16 Beck has "the vain display of property" instead of the "pride of life." Beck's translation is direct for v. 17: ". . . but if you do what God wants, you live forever."

The progress of thought in the text is as follows: In verse 15 John asks Christians not to love the world because love for the world and love for the Father cannot dwell in the same heart. Love of the world and love of the Father are incompatible, for the lusts and the vainglory of the world do not originate from the holy Father but from the sinful world (v. 17). The second reason John gives (v. 17) for not loving the world is that the world is already passing away with its lusts, but the person doing the will of God abides forever.

Amplifying Basic Concepts

What other portions of Scripture deal with this subject and what thoughts do these add?

Note the following passages: "Do not conform any longer to the pattern of this world, but be transformed by the renewing of your mind. Then you will be able to test and approve what God's will is—His good, pleasing and perfect will" (Rom. 12:2). "Religion that God our Father accepts as pure and faultless is this: to look after orphans and widows in their distress and to keep oneself from being polluted by the world" (James 1:27). Don't you know that friendship with the world is hatred toward God? Anyone who chooses to be a friend of the world becomes an enemy of God" (James 4:4).

In connection with verse 17 note the following passages: "Those who use the things of the world [should live] as not engrossed in them. For this world in its present form is passing away" (1 Cor. 7:31). "Whoever does God's will is my brother and sister and mother" (Mark 3:35).

What is the variation in meaning of this or that basic word in the rest of Scripture?

It is important to distinguish the different meanings of *kosmos* in the New Testament. In Romans 1:20 it refers to the ordered universe, in John 1:9 to the earth, in John 3:16 to the inhabitants of the earth, and in 1 John 2:15 to all that is alienated from God. John is referring not to the world as God first made it but to the world as the evil one, Satan, has corrupted it. The world in the sense of corrupt ungodly people hates us because we do not belong to their number (John 15:18-19).

How is the theological content of this text related to the whole of Biblical and confessional theology?

This text makes clear how Christians are to relate to the sinful world around them. Refusing to let love of the world displace love of the Father is a manifestation of the life Christians have in fellowship with the Father and with each other. The foundation of that fellowship is God's forgiveness of our sins (1 John 2:12). By faith we know the changeless, eternal Christ, who redeemed us. Why should we wish to conform to a changing evil world that is already passing away? We know the Father and His great love for us, by which we have become children of God. Why should we fall in love with the world, which can never satisfy as God's love can but will leave us only with remorse and hopelessness? Furthermore, by the power of God's Word abiding in us, we have in Christ already overcome the prince of this world (v. 14). Therefore in Christ we have the power to resist the world's enticements so as not to give in to its evil ways. The text is thus rooted ultimately in our relationship with the God of love. Out of that relationship flows our proper attitude toward the evil world.

The Central Thought

Love for the sinful world, which is passing away, is incompatible with love for the Father, through whom we abide forever.

Sermon Outline

Introduction: Pilate's priorities were power and prestige, but he would have neither if word got back to Rome that he couldn't keep order in his province. A riot was ensuing that had to be prevented at all costs. It didn't matter that Jesus was innocent of the charges brought against Him. What mattered was the preservation of Pilate's position. What the world had to offer was more important than truth and right.

Also for us, the things of the world sometimes become more important than the truth and treasures of God. The apostle John's warning against loving the world is also an urgent reminder that we are in

Outline :   **Lent: A Time for Renewal of Priorities**

I. We often let love for the world take priority over love for the Father.
   A. When the lust of the flesh tempts us,
      1. we choose to do evil and lose our integrity;
      2. we give in to base passions and rationalize sinful actions.
   B. When the lust of the eyes allures us,
      1. we cheat to assure success and advancement;
      2. we make possessions our gods.
   C. When the world's vainglory entices us,
      1. we make a display of our education, home, or achievements;
      2. we become too busy for God or His church.

II. It is foolish to let love for the world take priority over love for the Father.
   A. The desires of the flesh, the lust of the eyes, and the boastful vanity of the world are not from the Father.
      1. By going along with these features of the world, we accustom ourselves to a lifestyle that is shaped by the prince of this world and not by God.
      2. We place obstacles in the way of God's working in us to renew us.
      3. Deliberate and continuous loving of the world drives out love for the Father.
   B. The world is passing away, along with its lusts.
      1. Why should we wish to be part of a system that is already decaying?
      2. Why should we look for security in what is impermanent and can never really satisfy?

III. It is not necessary to let love for the world take priority over love for the Father.

A. We have been given power to do God's will by the Spirit, who has given us faith in God's grace.
   1. God demonstrated His love for us in Christ's suffering and death.
   2. God demonstrated His love for us by giving us faith in the Christ who made us the purpose of His life, death, and resurrection.
   3. God demonstrates His love for us by not letting us perish with the world but by keeping us forever with Him.
B. We can continue to do God's will by loving Him.
   1. We can love God rather than the evil world because God has enabled us to say: "For to me, to live is Christ and to die is gain" (Phil. 1:21).
   2. We can love God rather than the evil world because we have been crucified with Christ; it is no longer we who live, but Christ who lives in us; and the life we now live in the flesh we live by faith in the Son of God, who loved us and gave Himself for us (Gal. 2:20).

Conclusion: What a glaring contrast between Pilate and Jesus! Jesus' priority was to do God's will even though it led to suffering and death. It is time to renew our priorities, to bend our wills to Christ's will so that we do not love the world. When we seek first Christ's kingdom and His righteousness, all other things will be ours as well.

Sermon Illustrations

A beautiful motto was adopted by a college student: "I am willing to be third." He did not mean, of course, that he was casting away his ambitions and aspirations, content to loiter in the rear lines of action and achievement. Rather he meant that he would put the will of God first in his life, service to others second, and attention to himself last.

Wilbur E. Nelson, *Anecdotes and Illustrations* (Baker, 1971), p 21.

I never said not to love the world as My good creation, but I did say not to fall in love with evil things which divert your love from Me. Your self's desires, what you see and want, the things people are so proud of, those are all misdirected. Rather enjoy My creation, but focus your real desires on My desires for you, and I promise you will live forever.

Donald L. Deffner, *You Promised Me, God!* (CPH 1981), p. 94.

John Galsworthy in the *Forsyte Saga* records one of the ingrown Forsytes commenting proudly on his grandson: "What a bright boy he is," he fondly says, "to give a plugged sixpence to the beggar!" . . . God speaks to a child as surely as He spoke to Samuel in the tabernacle. When the child's responses to religious teachings are minimized and cut back and other things are given greater importance, it is like cutting back the branches and roots of a tree. The child asks for bread and is given the stone of material things, social events, or popularity—and thus the line of Byron applies: "This should have been a noble creature."

Nelson, p. 29.

In an old fable there was a magic skin the wearing of which would get a person everything he wished. But as each wish was granted the skin would shrink, and by the time the wearer got all that he wished for, the skin was so tight he could no longer breathe. . . . The magic skin is false ambition. Every time a false ambition is attended, a person shrinks. . . . False ambition [is] a short bed and narrow covering.

Nelson, p. 57.

How many times . . . there are voices clamoring from the outside: the many duties that are waiting, the problems we often feel we must think through, the interruptions by friends and neighbors. . . . And how many times does the outside voice get the preference and the prayer go neglected. . . . To be able to say, "You wait," to the outside voice and to attend first to prayer— what an achievement!

Nelson, p. 57.

It is easy for us to become sidetracked from our main purpose in life. We're like the man whom I recently saw in the Modern Museum of Art. All about him were great works of art by Rousseau, Gauguin, and Matisse. But he was standing peering through a small crack in a screen behind which some workmen were preparing the gallery for a new exhibit. He had come to the gallery to see great art hung under the best conditions of lighting and place. But he was sidetracked by the noises which the workmen were making as they worked. So we are placed in a world where our main business is to seek God and to see God. But we are sidetracked by the world's noises and our attention is diverted from Him by some fruitless venture. We become blind to his presence, and we cannot see His love. We peer through the cracks and openings and find nothing that can satisfy our soul's needs. We try to see everything but the One who can bring us the Kingdom.

An artist was one day sketching a landscape bathed in the soft light of the setting sun. In the foreground was a large barn. A friend watched him spend much time on the shingles of the barn. Finally the friend said, "If you spend so much time in painting the shingles on the barn, you won't have time to paint the sunset—and that is the big thing!" . . . So many people

50

spend all their time on the "shingles on the barn" and never get around to the glorious sunset. . . . People use all their time in pursuit of material things and that is all they get out of life. They miss the most important things.

Adapted from Nelson, p. 83

Let people call you eccentric because you are doing the will of God. Eccentric means nothing more than out of center, and if you have got a new center in God, of course you are out of the old center of the world. Let the world's machinery move around the old center. You have begun to move about quite another pivot than that around which the world moves. These words are . . . a splendid echo of those written by Paul . . . centuries ago: "Since, then, you have been raised with Christ, set your hearts on things above, where Christ is seated at the right hand of God. Set your minds on things above, not on earthly things. For you died, and your life is now hidden with Christ in God" (Col. 3:1–3).

Adapted from Nelson, p. 91.

Jesus said, "If anyone would come after me, he must deny himself and take up his cross and follow me." Like many of the "would be" disciples in Jesus' day we are quick to say how much we love the Lord and how deeply committed we are to Him. But when it comes to making the sacrifices of discipleship, our true commitment shows. Too often we are like the farmer who wrote to his girlfriend in town: "My dearest Abigail: No mountain is too high, no sea is too wide to keep me from your side. I would do anything to catch even one glimpse of you. Love Henry. P.S.: If it doesn't rain Saturday night, I'll try to drop by and say hello."

R. E. Lybrand, *Emphasis* 14, no. 4 (Sept. 1, 1984), p. 23

What, then, is this love of the world . . . ? It is anything in life that crowds Christ out. It is things that may in themselves be perfectly innocuous twining and twisting themselves about my soul, until I cannot reach up any longer to God. . . . It is anything that makes me forget, or even temporarily want to forget, that my citizenship is in heaven. It is anything that eliminates from my horizon the dimension of eternity. . . .

You may have met a man that tells you quite frankly that his greatest ambition in life is to make money. He may be an honorable man; he may indeed be doing a power of good. But that affluent life-style is his chief ambition. That is the love of the world. You have seen people conforming to convention til they were just fashion-ridden by the standards of a social set, their dominant passion being to keep up with their neighbors and to rise in the social scale. . . . That is the love of the world. I have heard of a family where a son, a brilliant student, felt moved to offer himself for missionary service, and the family said, "Drop it! Be sensible. Stay where you are!" That family was the entrenched principle of the love of the world.

James S. Stewart, *King Forever* (Abingdon, 1975), pp. 109–10.

One vision of what life with Christ can mean, one taste of that ampler, far more meaningful existence that is His gift, and we are never going to be content with the narrowness of an earthbound experience, with hopes unrealized and dissolving dreams. . . .

The only way ultimately to defeat the love of the world, to control a natural passion, is not to suppress it but to set against it a supernatural passion.

Stewart, p. 112

When a Roman recruit joined his legion, . . . he would say, lifting up his hand to heaven and taking the vow which was his "sacramentus," "I swear to follow the eagles of Caesar wherever they fly." And he knew what it meant—follow up to Hadrian's Wall and Caledonia, or down to the Ganges and the Nile, over the cold snows of Germany or the blazing sands of Africa— "I follow the eagles of Caesar!" . . . [Let us say]: "I follow Christ my king through light and dark, through life and death—I follow the King!"

Stewart, p. 113

We had guests. There were six of us at the table. When someone asked, "What time is it?" five people looked at their watches. I said, "Let's take count. How many watches or clocks do we have among us and in this house? There were two electric wall clocks, one radio clock, three alarm clocks, three wrist watches lying on a shelf (two needing repairs), one lovely Waltham given me by the faculty which I use only on travels or in the pulpit to help me stop. There were at least 11 in running order. I suspect most American homes may not be far behind.

How can we compare ourselves with the people of any other period in history, or for that matter, in almost any other part of the world?

We can accumulate more things, both in variety and quantity, than was ever dreamed of in earlier periods of history. In fact, we are virtually flooded with items, large and small. Like ours, the average home has more clocks than are ever needed to learn the time of day.

If we should be deluded into thinking we have found the secret of life by our command of things, we are being misled. We may have to unload in order to live. The cargo of our abundance may keep us fastened to earth. We may never see the stars nor scale the height.

The people of Jesus' day never had a chance at abundance. Yet even they were beguiled by the struggle for that which they could hold in their hands, however meager. Jesus warned them that something more was needed. . . .

The riches of the spirit or the heart will never come from listing an inventory of the things we possess. Such riches may be ours even if we have no list at all.

Alvin N. Rogness, *The Word for Every Day* (Augsburg, 1981), p. 115.

In the world of things the extraordinary quickly becomes the common-place. . . . I can remember the first automobile that came to our town, the first airplane I saw at a county fair, the first faint sounds from a radio. The first time I flew in a jet from Chicago to Los Angeles, I was exhilarated with our torpedo rise into the skies, but in a short time I fell asleep. . . . After we broke into space and we reached the moon, space flights were hardly mentioned in the press. I take the miracle of the computer for granted every time I am at an airport or a bank. Even the terrifying bomb I'm able to push back somewhere into the commonplace.

There is a world far more fascinating. That world is the kingdom of God. It can intersect, penetrate, invade, permeate everything we see and touch— and glorify it, if we will but let it. We can block it out of our consciousness. . . . We can remain blind and see no form. We can remain color-blind and see no color. We can live within the narrow walls of touch and measurement, or we can invite God to give us the gift of faith and have an incredibly rich world opened to us.

We were created for both worlds. We can love the winds that sing in the tree tops. We can love the lavish hues of a prairie sunset. We can love the soft touch of a grandchild's hand. A beautiful world yields its riches to our eyes, ears, and hands. Even the roar of the turbine may cheer us with the awareness of what man's science has achieved.

But there is another, a more fascinating world beyond our eyes and ears. There is a God we have never seen or touched or heard. He has established a kingdom in our midst, and, through Christ, has given us the right to enter.

Rogness, p. 189.

We are in the world, said Jesus, but not of the world. We march to a different drummer. We are to manage the world, but not by the standards of the world. We take our orders from Someone other than "the voice of the people." We are pilgrims and aliens, never naturalized in this world.

One of the perils for the Christian and for the church is to be swallowed up in the prevailing culture of their times. Today we need to be alarmed by the extent to which the Christian church has accepted the values of an all-too-permissive society, and has actually domesticated them under the rubric of "situational ethics."

... men and women live together without marriage, not clandestine but openly. Homosexuality, spoken about in whispers before, is often advocated as a licit option among Christian lifestyles. Divorce is taken for granted, and we now have liturgies for the dissolution of marriage covenants as well as for their making. Woe to the church that is both in the world and of it too!

Rogness, p. 279.

Lent: A Time for Renewal of Godly Fear

You did not receive a spirit that makes you a slave again to fear, but you received the Spirit of sonship. (Rom. 8:15)

Luke 23:39–43

Introduction

A cross is a strange place to look for renewal. Renewal implies a new beginning. Calvary signals an ending. Renewal implies hope, new possibilities, and new ways of living. Calvary signals hopelessness, regret, and the end of living. Yet if there is hope for renewal here, there is hope for renewal anywhere. If there is hope for renewal in a dying thief, there is hope for godly fear everywhere.

Fear as Terror

The one thief could still hear Pilate's words: "Guilty! Take him out and crucify him!" Those words probably did not come as a great surprise. He did not have to appear before the Sanhedrin before facing Pilate, for his was a criminal offense against Roman law, and he knew it. He also knew he was to die.

Like us, he had known all his life that he would die. We all share the knowledge that all our lives we are "held in slavery by [our] fear of death" (Heb. 2:15). We are like people living in a police state, who know that some day there will be a knock on the door in the dead of the night, and we will be summoned without warning to death. It's not *if*; it's *when*.

At the tomb of Lazarus Jesus was "deeply moved in spirit and troubled" (John 11:33). Then He wept. The Greek word conveying "deeply moved" carried the connotation of sadness mingled with rage, a deep indignation within Himself. That's certainly a clue to why Jesus wept. He knew that death—any death—was an abomination. Death was not the way that the Father intended us to go.

But there is no weeping for the thief. Even he admitted that he had it coming. To rescue some semblance of self-respect, he reached for his place in the pecking order. Even crosses, it would seem, have pecking orders. He was certainly bad, but this Jesus was worse. Even the spiritual leaders were taunting Him. So the thief and his partner joined in. To remove fear from himself, the thief transferred it to Jesus.

Then something happened. Perhaps it was what Jesus said, for when Jesus was reviled, the thief noticed that Jesus "did not retaliate; when he suffered, he made no threats. Instead, he entrusted himself to him who judges justly" (1 Peter 2:23). "Father," the thief heard Jesus say, "forgive them, for they do not know what they are doing." Somehow those words must have gotten through.

Now fear welled up in the thief's heart. This was a different kind of fear—not the fear of death or of the slow, agonizing suffering that could go on for hour after hour as his lungs filled with fluid, his blood drained slowly from his body, and the effects of dehydration slowly moved him toward death. He suddenly realized that he was in the presence of the Holy One. It wasn't Pilate's sentence of "Guilty! He must die!" It was *God's* sentence of "Guilty! He must die!" So the thief called out, "Don't you fear God, since you are under the same sentence? We are punished justly, for we are getting what our deeds observe. But this man has done nothing wrong."

The thief faced death with those words on his lips and the pronouncement of "guilty" accompanying him into eternity and taking him before God the Judge.

The sentence under which he now realized that he lived was God's sentence: "The soul who sins is the one who will die" (Ezek. 18:4). "The wages of sin is death" (Rom. 6:23). The world doesn't like to hear that. It smacks too much of fire and brimstone. Sweet Jesus wouldn't say that. God is love—that's the world's rationalizing theology of God. But the God of love does not show His love by excusing sin, for God is also just. If we spend our lives doing our will, ignoring the claim of God, and despising His presence, God will ultimately have to say: "Your will be done," and we will be "cast into the outer darkness" that Jesus described.

The thief heard the sentence from God, not Pilate, this time: "Guilty!" He knew that there had been another way to live, and he had chosen the low way. He had wasted an entire life. It didn't really matter that he was about to die shamefully on a cross. He could have been in a soft bed in an elegant room, surrounded by loving family and friends, and it would have been the same. He had wasted his life. He was afraid of facing God, of facing his wasted life.

When Fear Is Appropriate

To fear God is not always bad. The thief on the cross first had to experience fear of God in the sense of terror. He had to realize what he had spent his life avoiding: Life is lived in the presence of God. It doesn't matter what the world—our friends, family, co-workers—says is right or wrong, good or bad. God alone matters. When we realize at a moment of decision that we are in God's presence and that our choice will show whether we love God or the world and ourselves, that is good fear. It is godly fear. It is the voice of conscience. It is the only voice that our sinful desires will hear. Many times we have needed to say: "I cannot do this, for God is present. I cannot sin against the high and holy God." That is fear, and it is good fear.

Perhaps one of the reasons people make and break marriage vows so casually is that there is no fear of God in them. The same can be said of the many lifestyles that people pursue that lead nowhere except away from God. Maybe this is the contemporary preacher's fault. Maybe we have been proclaiming a casual religion about a God whose presence can be taken casually.

Perhaps another reason the fear of God is not present in so many people is that we have succumbed to pop psychology, which tends to remove guilt without confessing it, merely covering it up. Or maybe fear of God is missing because we preachers do more cheap moralizing in our sermons than we care to admit—dishing out heavy doses of shoulds and shouldn'ts with a quick recitation of Gospel and an even quicker Amen. Perhaps the proper fear of God is missing because people avoid—and maybe we help them avoid—listening to the "still, small voice" that hovers near and offers a personal, apart-from-everything-and-everyone-else confrontation with God.

All these reasons fell away for the thief, as they will for us, when death— that completely personal experience—is faced. But we dare not wait until then. That's why this Lent is "A Time for Renewal of Godly Fear" for us and our congregation. Part of that renewal must involve taking another look at our preaching and teaching. This is not a plea for pulpit-pounding, fire-and-brimstone preaching. It *is* a plea for recognizing the presence of God through a proclamation of true, honest, and complete Law and of lavish and wondrous grace.

But fear is not enough. The thief was now filled with godly fear—fear of God. But he needed more than fear, for in that fear he would soon die forever.

Fear as Slavery

In Romans 8:15 it becomes clear that fear (*phobos*) is not to be a master who takes us captive and keeps us in chains. Much of the resentment against legalistic religion is well founded, for it operates with fear as its motivation. When fear of God remains only terrified fear, guilt, failure, and sin are never removed, and consciences either die or people break free and enter another slavery: living without the proper fear of God. Here the preacher can probably think of and use numerous illustrations of people who lived under the burden of unrelenting fear until they finally heard the good news of complete freedom through Christ, whose perfect love "drives out fear" (1 John 4:18). Other examples suggest themselves: people whose fear of rejection was their motivation until one day they learned that the person they were trying to please loved them unconditionally. They had no reason to fear.

Fear Conquered

Until now, the thief had tried to transfer his fear to Jesus by reviling Him. But in a grand reversal of that transference, hope dawned. "If this man is innocent and yet is dying," he may have thought, "and if I am guilty and dying, I know why *I* am here. But why is *He* here? Could God be here in my fear, my guilt, and my death? Could God be here in order that my shame and guilt might indeed be transferred to Him? But how?" The thief couldn't get off the cross and place his life on Jesus' cross. He was nailed down and dying. He was helpless to act. He could not save himself. He could do only one thing. He could say: "Jesus, remember me when you come into your kingdom" (Luke 23:42). Remember *me!* Be here for *me!* Suffer here for *me!* Die here for *me!* Let your kingdom claim *me!*

Now the promise came back to him: "I tell you the truth, today you will be with me in paradise" (v. 43). The load of sin was lifted. The guilt was gone. The fear was gone. He would soon enter the presence of God with only these words on his lips: "I am guilty. I am not worthy to be called Your child. But Jesus died for me. He gave me the promise of paradise. I am here to collect on His promise." Soon he would hear the voice of the Father: "I know you. You are mine. Come, O blessed one. Enter the place prepared for you from eternity."

The thief is *not* the exception. This thief is our brother. He shows the rule by which we live and die and live eternally—the rule of grace and mercy by faith in Jesus Christ.

Fear as Sanctified Reverence

The thief spent what little time he had left—perhaps the four or five hours before the soldiers would come to break his legs and speed up his death— living in a new kind of godly fear. It is called the godly *reverence* of living in the Lord's presence. The cross became an altar of praise.

Jesus promised the kingdom to the thief, and the thief learned godly fear. That's the other side of godly fear—to know and believe that we live in the presence of God and His kingdom now and that we shall for eternity.

That's the gift of paradise. Paradise is not something we claim only at the end of our lives. It is something that claims us now. Paradise opens when we open God's Word. Paradise opens when we enter God's house. Paradise opens when we commune at the Lord's Table, for there God focuses His presence; Christ is there. Paradise opens when we realize that God is present to be reverenced in the decisions we make, in the people we serve, in the work we do, in the friends we love, in the families where He has placed us. Paradise *now* is not heavenly bliss. That will come in God's good time later. Paradise *now* is living in the Lord's presence at all times and in every circumstance. Wherever we are, God's holy name is present to be reverenced, obeyed, and celebrated.

Godly fear is the heart of the faithful ones—brothers and sisters of the thief on the cross—exclaiming with joy: "Lord, you remembered me! Help me to remember You!"

Sermon Outline

Introduction: Godly fear? Listen, I had enough fear of God in my church when I was a kid. I got so tired of it that I quit religion for a while. I don't want to go back to that!

Godly fear? That's incompatible with my concept of God. God is love! Why would I ever fear God? And why would I want to be renewed in godly fear? God is love. That's all I need to know about God.

Both of these reactions are typical of many people's response to the subject of godly fear. In the first instance, the fear of God is distorted. In the second, the love of God is misunderstood. Godly fear is not found, for example, only in the Old Testament while God's love is found in the New Testament. Both are found in both the Old Testament and the New. What is more, godly fear is found in the most fitting place—at the cross. We need godly fear. If we have ignored it or misused it or forgotten it, it must be retrieved and renewed. That's why we look this evening at

Outline :   Lent: A Time for Renewal of Godly Fear
 I. Godly fear as terror
   A. The thief lived without godly fear.
   B. Under the surface, fear is in every heart.
   C. The thief tried to transfer his fear.
   D. In Jesus he was confronted with God—and fear.
 II. Godly fear is appropriate
   A. when we realize we are in God's presence;
   B. when we realize our sinfulness and can no longer hide;
   C. when our old nature must be subdued.
III. Fear is slavery
   A. when terror is never relieved;
   B. when guilt remains.
IV. Fear is conquered
   A. when it is transferred to Christ;
   B. when forgiveness is proclaimed;
   C. when God's acceptance is believed.
 V. Fear is reverence
   A. when dying thieves reverence God;
   B. when even we can reverence, obey, and celebrate the presence of God.

Conclusion: Godly fear. Understood properly, we need it. We need it when we're tempted to sin, to stray, to make ourselves into gods. Godly fear leads us to reach for Him who removes the cause of fear and moves us into the godly fear of living reverence and praise.

Lent: A Time for Renewal of Christian Unity

*Is not the cup of thanksgiving for which we give thanks a
participation in the blood of Christ? And is not the bread
that we break a participation in the body of Christ?
Because there is one loaf, we, who are many, are one body,
for we all partake of the one loaf. (1 Cor. 10:16–17)*

Context

Paul's words in 1 Corinthians 10:16–17 occur in the larger context of his
discussion of eating food sacrificed to idols (8:1–11:1). In sacrifices to pagan
gods, only a part of the animal was offered to the deity; the rest was either
sold in the meat market or eaten in the idol's temple. Some Christians were
bothered about eating food that had been in such close contact with idolatry.
Paul was concerned that "strong" Christians, aware of their liberty in Christ,
would simply override the scruples of "weak" Christians by partaking freely
of meat offered to idols. Strong Christians were to remember that the line
between liberty and license is sometimes hard to draw, and that God's grace
does not work magically to keep a person from sinning. In 10:12 Paul presents the Old Testament Israel as a warning. Of course, God is faithful (v.
13) and will strengthen Christians to resist temptation. At the same time,
Christians must be alert to situations in which their behavior might give
both other Christians and unbelievers the impression that it is not wrong
to sacrifice to idols. Idolatry must be avoided at all costs.

Paul's point in verses 16–17 is that communion with Christ in the Lord's
Supper is "total and exclusive and makes any other communion a communion with *demons*" (Martin Franzmann, *Concordia Self-Study Commen-
tary* [CPH, 1979], New Testament, p. 153). Christians know from the Lord's
Supper how deeply they participate in Christ. They also know from the Old
Testament Scriptures that the priests who ate the sacrifices were by that
act sharers in the altar and of the God whose presence the altar signified
(v. 18). Thus the Corinthian Christians could judge for themselves how
inconsistent any form of idolatry would be with their participation in Christ.
Paul argues from the Old Testament principle that every sacrifice not offered
to God is being offered to demons (Deut. 32:17, 37). The *koinōnia* that
the Christian enjoys in the Lord's Supper simply does not permit cultic
fellowship with demons.

Notes on the Text

Although Paul's reference to the Lord's Supper in 1 Corinthians 10:16–17
occurs in connection with his discussion of pagan sacrificial meals, Paul
does not describe the Lord's Supper as a Christian sacrificial meal. Partaking

of bread and wine is *koinōnia,* a union or sharing in the blood and body of Christ. The exalted Christ is identical with the human, historical Christ who had body and blood.

Paul refers to the wine of the Lord's Supper as "the cup of thanksgiving" (v. 16 NIV; RSV: "blessing"; Greek: *eulogia*). It will always be a cup of blessing or thanksgiving because Christ gave thanks (*eucharisteō,* 11:24) when He blessed it at the first celebration of the Supper. We in turn give thanks and bless it when we speak the words that Jesus Himself used at the institution of the Lord's Supper. By so doing we consecrate the bread and the wine for use in the Lord's Supper, that is, for sacramental and not just ordinary use. Speaking of the bread, Paul says that we break it, which refers to distributing the bread to the communicants and their eating it. Paul thus emphasizes the necessity of the consecration and distribution if communicants are to share in the body and blood of Christ. In such consecrated and distributed bread and wine communicants receive their incarnate, redeeming Lord, for He is truly present in the bread and wine. The bread is the body of Christ, and the wine is the blood of Christ.

In 10:17 Paul makes clear that the community that partakes of the sacrament is inwardly related to Christ who in wine and bread is really and effectively present. Furthermore, not only do communicants share in Christ's body and blood and therefore in all the benefits that His crucified body and shed blood secured for them, but they also have a sharing or union with one another. Partaking of one bread creates fellowship between the communicants, merging them into one body. On verse 17 Martin Chemnitz says: "In the Supper I do not receive a particular body and you a different one, but we all receive the one and the same body of Christ along with the bread, in accordance with the words. And because in this way the members of the church are joined together in the one body of Christ, therefore they are also joined with one another and become one body, whose Head is Christ. . . . For through the bread we are united with the body of Christ, and through the body with Christ Himself, and through Christ with the Father. Thus we are made partakers with the Father, the Son, and the Holy Spirit" (Martin Chemnitz, *The Lord's Supper,* trans. J. A. O. Preus [CPH, 1979], p. 143). "Because Christ in the Supper joins Himself most intimately to us . . . by His body and blood, at the same time through this assumed nature of His, which is akin to ours, He will work powerfully and efficaciously in the believers, so that . . . we also may be members of one another" (ibid., p. 193). All who partake of the one sacramental bread, which is Christ's body, are thereby made one spiritual body.

Homiletical Helps

Central Thought: Holy Communion is a blessed meal that lets us participate in Christ's body and blood so that we are joined to Christ and to each other.

Goal: The hearers will commune often for renewal in their unity in Christ and in each other.

Problem: Our yearning for communion sometimes wanes because we prefer renewal in sin to renewal in Christ.

Means: Participation in Christ's body and blood is participation in forgiveness and life.

Sermon Outline

Introduction: St. Paul in 1 Corinthians 12 uses the analogy of a human body to describe the unity in diversity of the church. He speaks of the body as one even though it has many members. Just so, although Christians are individuals with different abilities and tasks, they nevertheless form one body.

Yet because of our differences, we are not always conscious of our unity, and we have difficulty expressing it. The meal we partake of tonight is a means of expressing and renewing our unity. As we look more closely at what Paul is saying, may the Holy Spirit bless our thoughts and words and actions and make

Outline : Lent: A Time for Renewal of Christian Unity
 I. In our common Lord
   A. The Lord is Christ, who unites Himself with us in the bread and the wine of Holy Communion.
     1. We take into ourselves His true body and blood.
     2. We participate intimately in God Himself.
   B. Such participation in Christ excludes participation in idolatry.
     1. By worshiping the gods of money, prestige, and sex we divorce ourselves from Christ (1 Cor. 6:15–16; Jer. 3:19–20).
     2. God will have no other gods before Him (Zech. 1:14).
It is time for renewal in our common Lord so that we can be done with those things that usurp Christ's place within.
 II. In our common blessings
   A. Christ blesses us with His forgiveness.
     1. We need forgiveness for our unfaithfulness, an unfaithfulness that can never satisfy (Ezek. 16:28).
     2. We receive full and free forgiveness, for Christ gave His body and His blood to secure that forgiveness. This assuages our guilt and calms our conscience (Ps. 65:4; 107:9; Jer. 31:14).
   B. Christ blesses us with abundant life (John 10:10).
     1. We need Christ's life because we live in bodies that will die.
     2. We receive the life of Jesus, over whose body death no longer has dominion (Rom. 6:9).
It is time for renewal in our common blessings so that the life of Jesus may be manifested in our mortal bodies (2 Cor. 4:10–11).
 III. In our common task
   A. We confess the faith.
     1. We make a united affirmation of the real presence of Christ in Holy Communion.

2. We unanimously confess all that Christ has taught (Matt. 28:20).
B. We share joys and sorrows (1 Cor. 12:26).
C. Standing against Satan.
1. We will not be such easy prey for Satan when we remain in fellowship with each other.
2. We can better resist Satan when we strengthen our fellowship by partaking of Holy Communion (Acts 2:42).

It is time for renewal in our common task so that we will be a body of Christians who together confess Christ, support one another, and stand firm against temptation.

Conclusion: Come and partake of Holy Communion. It is time for renewal of our Christian unity in a common Lord, common blessings, and a common task.

Sermon Illustrations

The evening meal was ended. The men in the fraternity sat back in their chairs, moved away from the table and prepared to listen to the speaker for the evening. He was a pastor at one of our ... campus churches, and he had been asked to speak about problems of students as he sees and hears them. When he concluded his comments, the subject was thrown open for discussion. A question came up which was one that [is] asked in almost every fraternity or sorority or dormitory. . . . "Pastor, do you ever think there will be *one* church?"

When [he] replied, "There already *is* only one church," the men smiled. Evidently they thought [he] meant the Lutheran denomination.

That question: "Do you ever think there will be one church?" goes down to the heart of what the church actually is . . . [John 10:11–16], implies that if we're going to think about this lesson, we can't escape asking ourselves, "What in the world, and what under heaven, actually is the Christian church?"

From a sermon by Edward Wessling. Quoted by Donald L. Deffner in *For Example* (CPH, 1977), p. 48.

Auguste Rodin, the French sculptor, invited his friends and students to examine his statue of Balzac. One student exclaimed: "What hands! I've never seen such marvelous hands before!" Another student's reaction was much the same. "Those hands," he said, "they are alive!" A third cried: "Those hands! If you had never done anything else, they would make you immortal!" Rodin's response was totally unexpected. He seized an axe and with supernatural strength chopped off the hands which had elicited such extravagant praise. He said: "I was forced to destroy those hands because they had a life of their own. They didn't belong to the life of the composition.

Remember this, and remember it well. No part is more important than the whole!"

Adapted from Wilbur E. Nelson, *Anecdotes and Illustrations* (Baker, 1971), p. 43.

My church is torn by factionalism. Some say we are baptized *into* the name of the Father, others hold that it is *in* the name of the Father. I belong to one of these groups, and I feel very strongly about it. In fact, I'd die to uphold the opinion of our group—but for the life of me I can't remember which one it is.

David Lloyd George; quoted in Albert P. Stauderman, *Let Me Illustrate* (Augsburg, 1983), p. 42.

Unity and common purpose are hard to find anywhere in the world. Despite its name, the United Nations is far from united; rarely has there been a unanimous decision on any major item. Statesmen build walls and erect barriers around their countries, and the world is divided by curtains of iron or bamboo. Even in the Christian congregation people of diverse ideas, backgrounds, and beliefs come together, and one wonders what common purpose they possess. What draws a congregation together? There's just one common interest: The unifying force is their faith. It provides a core of purpose for their varied lives and enables them to work together in harmony.

Stauderman, p. 167.

The Arabian Nights fable of Sinbad the sailor describes a magnetic rock in the Indian Ocean that draws all the nails and bolts out of passing ships until the ships collapse and sink. In a sense the passing of time and the distracting influences of the world loosen the nails and bolts that hold us together in families and communities. We need constant renewal to tighten up the unity of fellowship in the ties of faith.

Stauderman, p. 167.

Watching a symphony orchestra perform can help us understand the need for accepting our place in life and doing our best with it. The violinists may fiddle furiously throughout an entire selection, the cymbals crash only once or twice, the soft woodwinds are barely heard, while the brasses blare out from time to time, yet all form part of a beautiful whole. If the cymbals dominated the entire piece, it would be a horrible noise. If it were all violins, it would be unbalanced. All must fit together, playing their parts. For the skinny little piccolo to envy the big fat tuba or for the bass viol to cover the violin's part would not be useful. Harmony comes only with the blending of a variety of gifts—if all are playing in the same key and all are playing the same piece.

Stauderman, p. 168.

We begin at the wrong end, in this business of Christian unity, if we follow the pattern of the world and think first in terms of bigger and bigger mergers in order to meet our competition in the ideological struggle. We don't reach Christian unity by riding roughshod over sincere convictions and trying to create, with all possible speed, a super church to confront the Goliaths of the modern world. We begin by realizing again what we have so often forgotten—that God has given a unity to his Church. We *are* all one in Christ Jesus. When St. Paul found, as he often did, a spirit of division and faction in one of his young churches, this is what he spoke about—their fundamental unity in Christ . . . this is where we begin. God sees his Church as one.

David H. C. Read, *Sons of Anak* (Charles Scribner's Sons, 1964), pp. 34–35.

In our Christian creeds we confess that we belong to the *one* church, "the one, holy, Christian (or catholic) and apostolic church." How can we speak of *one* church, when we belong to the Lutheran, the Baptist, the Methodist, or Episcopal church? P. T. Forsythe, eminent British theologian, in his book *The Church and the Sacraments* attempts an answer:

I will offer an illustration. When strangers come to Cambridge and when they have seen the colleges, it would be natural to say, "Now take me to the University." It is a puzzling request. The Senate House—it is not there. The Library—it is not there. The Schools—it is not there either. It has a personality of its own; it is not a mere group, or sum, or amalgam. It has a history, a tradition, a life, a power, a spell, which is not simply the added-up history of the colleges. To the curious stranger you cannot show the University—which yet is Cambridge. Who can deny the University? It is a great reality, a great spiritual reality, in which its colleges inhere. It gives the colleges their true value. It is that which they serve. It is the one spiritual corporation in which . . . the colleges hold together. It dignifies them all. It is the mother of them from above.

So it is with the true Church. The universal Church is, so to say, the University of the churches . . . they are true churches in proportion as they hold of this spiritual reality, which is their life.

Quoted in Alvin N. Rogness, *The Word for Every Day* (Augsburg, 1981), p. 244.

Sometimes we Christians forget that we belong to a larger group than the Christian church. We are human beings before we are white, black, yellow, brown, or red, before we are from West or East, before we are Christian, Buddhist, or Moslem.... We are one great human family.... Those of us who have allowed Christ to capture us are in a special group within the larger family, the body of Christ on earth, the church. We are one with all humanity; we are one with all Christ's followers.

We often deny both of these unities. We divide into nations, races, creeds, cultures—and look across these fragile and illusory borders as if we are strangers and enemies.... A crisis does tend to make us forget our differences. A tornado, a typhoon, a flood suddenly bring all into a fellowship of danger and suffering. In disaster a rich man's son, a poor man's son, a white and a black, coping side by side, become friends, their differences forgotten.

God must love diversity. We know he loves unity.... He wants us all to be ... concerned for one another, serving one another, and growing to love one another.

Rogness, p. 355.

For the apostle Paul there could be no real participation in the Lord's Supper where there was no real unity of spirit and behavior among the participants.... It is going beyond the biblical evidence to argue as some do that the celebration of the Supper actually creates unity. The fellowship in the Lord by the Spirit must be there already as a necessary presupposition. But there is surely enough in the passages in 1 Cor. and elsewhere (Acts 2:42) to permit us to conclude that the unity and fellowship which we experience in Christ through the Holy Spirit will find an important, divinely ordained expression in the celebration of the Lord's Supper; and hence that the Supper is a significant means for the strengthening of Christian fellowship.

Bruce Milne, *We Belong Together—The Meaning of Fellowship* (InterVarsity Press, 1978), p. 68.

You cannot have the head without the body. The Christ who comes to us is a Christ who comes clothed with his body. We cannot therefore expect to grow in relationship with him if we are all the while careless of our relationships with his people. We cannot accept the head and reject the body. Our relationships with the members of our local fellowship will be a factor of real significance for our spiritual growth. In the Lord's Supper these two dimensions are drawn explicitly together.

Milne, p. 69.

We need to take the horizontal dimension of the Supper very seriously. One of the results of our loss of this aspect has been the development of an approach to the Supper which is highly individualistic. People even talk sometimes of "making my communion," and the whole thing becomes an individualistic, pious act undertaken by the individual as an expression of their personal devotion to the Lord. Without wishing to minimize what such practice means to those who engage in it, we can surely point out on the basis of the New Testament that such an understanding falls short of Scripture, and is even a serious misunderstanding. The Lord's Supper is an act of the *whole* church. It is an act of the congregation, and it is in such a context that it needs consciously to be celebrated. We need to avoid allowing sentimental associations to determine our biblical and theological interpretation.

Milne, p. 70.

Good Friday

Lent: A Time for Renewal of Faith

They are justified freely by his grace through the redemption that came by Christ Jesus. God presented him as a sacrifice of atonement, through faith in his blood. (Rom. 3:24–25)

Is. 53:3–6; Luke 23:44–49

Notes on the Meaning of the Text

Romans 3:24 is God's answer to the hopeless situation described in verse 23, namely that all people have sinned and therefore fall short of the glory or approbation that God would give to the sinless. The status of human beings under sin makes it impossible for God to approve of them when He acts according to His law. If human beings are to have a new status, it can come about only through God's action, and God has acted "apart from law" (Rom. 3:21). What God did, according to verse 24, was to announce an acquittal that violates all legal justice. God found a way to declare people righteous despite their universal sinfulness, something they in no way deserve. God's acquittal is a gift (*dōrean*); it is free, without cost to the sinner. God's acquittal is by grace (*chariti*), by gratuitous favor and without reserve. But God did not simply ignore sin; He dealt with it as the God of justice. His freely given acquittal is based on the redemption (*apolutrōseōs*) that God Himself provided in Christ Jesus. So God's grace was costly. He had to ransom human beings from their ruined past by nothing less than the precious blood of Christ.

The word *hilastērion* in verse 25 refers to the cover of the ark of the covenant in the Old Testament tabernacle. This cover was sprinkled with blood and hid the accusing Law. Once a year, on the great Day of Atonement, the high priest alone entered the Holy of Holies to sprinkle the blood on the cover of the ark. It is significant that this highest expiatory act of the Old Testament now typifies Christ's expiation. God set forth Christ as the perfect expiation through His blood for all sins of all people. Through Christ's death on the cross a once-for-all justification is available to all through faith (*dia pisteōs*). The saving act on the cross and the personal apprehension of it belong directly together. What God has given to the world in Christ can be received only by faith. God's acquittal is infinitely great and absolutely free, but it does not benefit the person who does not by faith receive it. When God now justifies a person who has faith in Jesus there is no room for human merit. There is room only for the faith that receives God's justification and gives glory to God.

The Text and the Good Friday Service

On Good Friday we remember the event by which our redemption was secured. On the cross Jesus shed His blood and was thereby put forward by God as the final and perfect expiation for sin, an expiation to which all the Old Testament sacrifices pointed. At the cross God's love and justice met so that neither denied the other. The cross was God's way of bringing about His approbation of sinful human beings in a way that was not sentimental or arbitrary. Good Friday affords us an opportunity to focus sharply on the supreme demonstration of God's love: the atonement by His Son, which brought about our deliverance from sin and our reconciliation with God. The text also points us to the need in the Good Friday service of renewing our grasp on Jesus as the expiation for our sins and the basis of our acceptance by God. Only through what Jesus accomplished on the cross on Good Friday has salvation become a reality for us.

An examination of Renewal in Relation to Faith

Is there a need for renewal in relation to faith?

We tend to make faith a work of the law

when we equate faith with self-surrender to God;

when we equate faith with a certain degree of intellectual understanding;

when we require of ourselves a certain amount of courage, boldness, or calmness as proof of faith;

when we associate lack of physical health and material success with weak faith;

when we make a particular level of holiness of life a criterion of saving faith;

when we think that faith is something we must do to fulfill a requirement for salvation;

when we think that both faith and works are necessary for salvation.

Faith can be renewed

by listening to God's assurance in His Word of our justification by grace as a gift;

by contemplating the redemption that Jesus accomplished for us on the cross;

by remembering that God bestowed His grace on us in baptism;

by partaking of Christ's body and blood in Holy Communion.

When faith is renewed

we quit trying to decide for Christ and live each day in the decision that God in Christ has made for us;

we quit trying to meet certain conditions and start trusting in God's promises;

we quit looking so much at ourselves and direct our attention to Christ and our neighbor;

we quit trying to get God to love us and realize that we can't do anything to stop God from loving us;

we quit trying to get God to accept us and realize that God accepts us as we are.

Sermon Outline

Introduction: We are familiar with the details surrounding the event we commemorate today. The raising of the crosses, the crucifixion of Jesus and the two robbers, Jesus' words as He hung on the cross, His painful, gory death—all these we have heard about in the Scripture readings from the Passion accounts.

Our purpose today is not to rehearse the Good Friday event but to focus on its meaning for us. Our text from Paul's letter to the Romans will help us do that. The apostle spells out the meaning of Christ's death, a meaning that only faith can grasp. That's why this day is indeed

Outline :   **Lent: A Time for Renewal of Faith**
I. On this day Christ expiated our sin.
   A. Sin's penalty had to be paid.
      1. God's justice demanded it.
      2. Atonement had to be made before sinners could be approved by God.
   B. Christ's blood alone could expiate our sins.
      1. As God's innocent Lamb, Christ atoned for all sin.
      2. We can believe that our sins were included in this atonement.
II. On this day Christ redeemed us.
   A. His blood was the ransom price.
      1. This ransom was sufficient.
      2. This ransom God accepted.
   B. We were thereby delivered.
      1. We are freed from the punishment of sin.
      2. We are freed from the burden of having somehow to redeem ourselves.
III. On this day Christ made it possible for God to justify us.
   A. Because of what Christ did, God declares us righteous.
      1. God does so by grace.
      2. God's declaration is an unconditional gift.
   B. We can believe that we are included in God's declaration.
      1. God accepts us as we are.
      2. God regards us as righteous because Christ's righteousness has been imputed to us.

Conclusion: Good Friday is a time for renewal of faith because the meaning of Christ's death can be grasped only by faith. As we focus on what happened on Christ's cross, the Holy Spirit assures us that our sin has been atoned for, our redemption accomplished, our justification declared. We don't ever have to doubt these benefits of Christ's death. Because Jesus rose from the dead, we can live each day in the certainty of the cross-earned grace of God.

Sermon Illustrations

When a ship was crossing a stormy bay, the engine suddenly stopped, and for a few minutes the situation was one of peril. A woman rushed up to the captain and asked anxiously, "Is there any danger?" "Madam," the captain replied, "we must trust in God." "Oh," she wailed, "has it come to that?"

Terence E. Johnson, *Emphasis* 14, no. 4 (Sept. 1, 1984), p. 22.

Our world has seen a veritable explosion of knowledge in all areas. Who could have dreamed a few short years ago that we would conquer smallpox, place men on the moon, and live with the magic of the computer?

But it's not knowledge that provides life with ultimate meaning. It is faith. We must have something—or someone—to believe in. Knowledge is made up of a vast assortment of pieces, like a jigsaw puzzle. It is faith that can assemble the pieces into a picture of the whole.

Alvin N. Rogness, *The Word for Every Day* (Augsburg, 1981), p. 55.

Jesus said: "You believe in God; believe also in me." When you do, you stake your life on the God that Jesus revealed and that Jesus Christ is. . . .

If you have gone this far—better still, been taken this far by the Holy Spirit—you have plunged into a way of life which will dominate everything you think and do. You rest in a strange peace which nothing else in the world can give you. You stand on the solid ground which is still there if the planet blows up.

Adapted from Rogness, p. 120.

This is the characteristic attitude of the man of faith in every age—not stoicism, not fantasy nor credulity, nor muddle-headed, pious rhetoric that builds its house of life precariously on the sands of sentiment, but solid, basic realism with its roots right down to the everlasting rock—. . . in Christ we have seen . . . the very heart of God made plain. Can we distrust a love that blazed out in the flame of Calvary? Can we disbelieve the power that turned that tragic hour to triumph? Can we forget how at one point after another of the road we have traveled, the everlasting mercy has come to meet us—all the way back beyond our earliest memories to our very birth and baptism? What was that baptism of yours but God in Christ promising to be with you even to the end of the world? Luther, at one dark period of his life, was being tempted by the devil of discouragement, but when he had nothing else to hang on to . . . he kept repeating as his last defiance . . .

"I have been baptized!"—as though to say, "Nothing can alter that! God will never be less loving than when in baptism Christ's name was sealed upon me."

James S. Stewart, *King Forever* (Abingdon, 1975), pp. 101–02.

What about our present faith? Is it the faith the Bible speaks of—central, basic, controlling? Or is it a side bet that we make with life, hedging against the possible failure of our ambitions? Or is it a means to a very secular end—a therapeutic device to bring us greater poise and effectiveness?

The test is the test of Job. In that dramatic prologue we hear the sneer of Satan: "Doth Job serve God for nought?" Men will trust in God only for what they can get out of it in the way of prosperity, happiness, and success. This satanic theology is still with us. The answer of the book of Job is to show us a man . . . tempted to "curse God and die," ready to argue with the Almighty, but still, still retaining his basic faith expressed at its noblest in the climactic words: "Though He slay me, yet will I trust in Him."

David H. C. Read, *I Am Persuaded* (Charles Scribner's Sons, 1961), pp. 100–01.

God has the responsibility for what He has said—even for my faith. For everything else grows hazy and blurred, especially my pious resolutions. The one thing that stands secure and solid is this promise: you shall live. I stake everything on this card. God declares that He has it in His hand. So He has the responsibility. In His name I cast myself into the night and hope that I shall fall into the hands of God. . . . Faith has such moments . . . when it shuts its eyes and lets itself fall, moments when it knows that now it's either the abyss or the hand of God, when it dares to take the leap solely because God has said the Word, knowing despite everything to the contrary, that it can end, not in the abyss, but only in the hands of God.

Helmut Thielicke, *Christ and the Meaning of Life* (Baker, 1975), pp. 124–25.

A feeling of weakness under a heavy load is not a lack of faith, but is just that, a feeling. . . . Faith may be very strong when emotions are very low.

Faith is based on the reliable witness of the Scriptures. . . . Supernatural alterations of my circumstances are not necessary for my faith to be strong. In fact, true faith holds steady when it seems that nothing is going well.

Charles Durham, *Temptation—Help for Struggling Christians* (InterVarsity Press, 1982), pp. 112–13.

A steamer crossing the Atlantic had two compasses. One was in the usual place at the wheel, the other was halfway up one of the masts. There it was not affected by the large amount of iron in the framework of the vessel. Whenever the compasses differed, the helmsman steered by the higher compass. So it is as we move through the sea of life. There is the compass of feeling affected by all the chances and changes of the world around us, all the whims and doubts and variations within us. This compass is unreliable; it will send us onto the rocks. But we have a higher compass—that of faith.

Wilbur E. Nelson, *Anecdotes and Illustrations* (Baker, 1971), p. 85.

A friend of mine tells of how, years ago, he was in a horrible car accident. His car was totaled, and he woke up for the first time after the crash in a hospital bed. There was no one in the room at the time, so he felt himself gingerly all over and then looked around the room. Over on the window sill was a chart and he carefully got out of bed and walked over to look at it. He read his name, and then "Condition: critical." Me? Critical? he thought. He crept even more carefully back to bed and leaning back slowly took stock of his situation. "Well, there's absolutely nothing I can do about it. So I throw myself completely in your hands, Lord. Do what you wish." He says he never felt such a complete sense of relief and joyful daring as he took the "leap of faith" into God's hands and laid back to relax in the safe care of the everlasting arms.

He calls that feeling, which he has sought to practice throughout his life, his "theology of failure." In life's circumstances you trust, you leap, you dare to fail, to lose, to miss out. But at least in God's name, you dared.

Donald L. Deffner, *Bound to Be Free* (Morse Press, 1981), p. 117.

Few people know that the Gloria Patri ("Glory be to the Father and to the Son, and to the Holy Ghost") which many of us sing in our churches every Sunday was really based on the death-march song of the early Christian martyrs. They knew they would die, but they faced their end with conviction, knowing "whom they had believed and . . . persuaded that he was able to keep that which they had committed unto him against that day."

Deffner, p. 118.

It has been my experience that those who doubt more than they believe try to subject God to the limits of their own reason. They want God on their terms, according to their own rationale. They seem to say that if they were God, things would have been done differently. And right here . . . is the crux of the problem. They see themselves as God. For to be wiser than God is to be God. If we really want to get to know God, it is better to begin with faith. What we really need is a faith that seeks understanding rather than an understanding that seeks faith. To put it another way, "In doubt? Faith it!" No matter how little our faith might be—even if it is smaller than a mustard seed—God is saying . . . that there is great potential for its growth.

John H. Krahn, *Seasonings for Sermons* (CSS, 1983), 3:63.

I cannot argue myself into [faith]. Nor can I achieve it by moral effort and religious conflict of conscience. But it is manifested to me out of the history of Christ, and I find a continual witness in people and events around about me. To put it simply: God is for me; I am his child. Christ is beside me; I am his brother. Whether this makes me believe more strongly or whether I doubt all the more, whether I'm swallowed up in the darkness of night or find myself at the dawn of a new day—I know: there is Someone waiting for me, who will not give me up, who goes ahead of me, who lifts me up, Someone to whom I am important.

Jürgen Moltmann, *Experiences of God* (Fortress Press, 1980); quoted in *Church Management— The Clergy Journal* (January 1982), p. 22.

A minister tells of a woman, a happy and efficient wife of a fellow pastor, who was experiencing her full share of life's sunshine and shade, but with no real darkness falling her way. And then, suddenly, without warning, her husband died of a heart attack, leaving her terribly alone and afraid; afraid of her own decisions, afraid of the present, afraid of the future.

When the minister visited his colleague's wife, he related how she was in the vicelike grip of fear—so tyrannized that most of her time was spent in bed. She was so terrified that she became bedridden.

When the minister saw her two years later, he was pleasantly surprised to find a poised, serene woman, working as a receptionist in an insurance office. When the pastor asked her to explain her amazing recovery, the woman replied, "The work helped, of course, but I couldn't work at all until I faced my fear and saw it was basically a selfish rebellion against God and what I thought was God's will. When I saw that, I began to pray that God would forgive my selfishness. And as I prayed, I became aware of God's hand reaching down to me, and I somehow began to reach up in faith until I finally clasped that hand. And then to my amazement, I found His hand clasping mine; and I knew that He really cared and that He would help me as long as I held His hand in faith."

Donald L. Deffner, *Sermon Illustrations for the Gospel Lessons* (CPH, 1980), p. 25

Easter: A Time for Renewal of Hope

Put your hope in the LORD, *for with the* LORD *is unfailing love and with him is full redemption. (Ps. 130:7)*

Matthew 28:1–10; Psalm 130

Introduction

If you choose to use the liturgy prepared for the Easter celebration, you will note that it contains a highly unusual element. Instead of a sanctuary filled with lilies and Easter banners, the sanctuary is as barren of color as it was on Good Friday. The cross is still veiled. The lights in the nave are dimmed. If the organ is playing at all, it is playing somber selections.

There are reasons for this. One is pragmatic. How often haven't you begun an Easter service by shouting at your people the words of triumph, "JESUS CHRIST IS RISEN TODAY!" only to be greeted with the drowsy, mumbled response: "He is risen 'deed." So you try again, "HE IS RISEN!" The reply comes back: "Hall-lou-yuh." In exasperation you shout: "HE IS RISEN IN-DEED!" They respond, "He is ris'n 'ndeed, hall-lou-yuh." That's one reason for the somber church. Sleepy people aren't ready for Easter's shocking surprise any more than the women were who first went to the tomb.

That leads to the second reason for this suggested change from an ordinary Easter. Historically and theologically, the barren altar more accurately portrays the way that Easter first happened. What occurred on Easter morning happened *out of* gloom and death and hopelessness. The triumph of Easter morning began in defeat. That gloom and defeat and hopelessness and death were ours. Only when we know how hopeless life is when it is lived in the absence of God, only when we know how deadly is life without the living God, only when we know how truly tragic life is when it is lived without the joy of resurrection will we know how to live in joyous, lively hope. Peter writes, "Praise be to the God and Father of our Lord Jesus Christ! In his great mercy he has given us new birth into a living hope through the resurrection of Jesus Christ from the dead" (1 Peter 1:3). That living hope is ours. But first we must go with the women to the tomb, not expecting the surprise of joy but the gloom of defeat and death and hopelessness.

Out of the Depths

The prayer of the psalmist from Psalm 130 could easily have been the prayer on the lips of Jesus' followers on Holy Saturday and Easter morning. Only when you and I stand at an ending, at a death—physical or emotional—can we understand this prayer. How high is high? How deep is the depth? You can answer that only when you've stood in between and *know* you were there. The disciples of Jesus had stood with *Him*. They had been on the heights with the One who came in the name of the Lord. They had seen how high love is, for Jesus had stooped down to the lowly, the crippled and hurting, the rejected and outcast, and lifted them up. They had seen how high hope could be, for He had told them of the kingdom of God, and He had promised them that "in my Father's house are many rooms" (John 14:2). They had seen how high they could stand, for He had pointed them to the lilies and birds of contentment, the basin and towel of service, and the arms of God that beckoned to them. They caught a glimpse of how high is high when Jesus was transfigured.

When you have been on the heights, anything less is low indeed. Now their Lord of hope was laid low in death. Those were the depths—the depths of love conquered, hope dashed, promises withdrawn, and death a certainty. Most of all, if God could not bring hope, if the sinless Son of God could not conquer, how could they? His death was the death of hope. Now evil would become accepted, trial would be meaningless, "luck" would be the reason for good fortune, and "the breaks" would be the answer to misfortune. Life would not only be in control of the conquering, evil one; it would be out of control with no direction, no purpose, no hope, no reason to fight back. The entire theme of the Lenten series, dealing with renewal, would be a farce if Jesus Christ had only died on the cross and was still in a sealed tomb. Renewal cannot happen if the One who came to bring the renewal is just like anyone else, placed into a tomb, and conquered by the old enemy called death.

The psalmist had not given up, even in the depths, for "out of the depths" he was reaching up to the God who is there. "O Lord, hear my voice. Let your ears be attentive to my cry for mercy" (Ps. 130:2).

Here the preacher must ask some questions both about his congregation and about himself. What characterizes the people whom we serve? Do they live as if they are still in the pre-Easter gloom? Is their vision so low that they shuffle through life, only marking time in the here and now? Does life consist in what they accumulate? Is their love only self-love for "me" and "mine"? Is there no anger at what is and no yearning for what should be and shall be? Have they simply made their peace with the world and joined it? Are they living without the vision of the kingdom and apart, in any meaningful way, from the King? Are they living as though Jesus did not rise from the dead to give them a living hope? Then before the Easter message can be heard, they need to go to the tomb today and pray with the psalmist, "If you, O LORD, kept a record of sins, O Lord, who could stand?" (Ps. 130:3).

Keeping a Record of Sins

"Keeping a record of sins" suggests someone with a ledger who marks down every sin that we have committed. The One who marks is not convinced by our rationalizations, nor is He impressed by our insistence that we are not as bad as Mr. A or Mrs. B. The One who marks the ledger knows the secret that we try to avoid—that we sin against God, that we are accountable to the Holy One.

The hymn writer is correct as he takes us to the cross, points, and declares: "You who think of sin but lightly, nor suppose the evil great, here may view its nature rightly, here its guilt may estimate."

The Lord is the One who knows. Without the cross the ledger stands, and we are condemned. "If you, O Lord, kept a record of sins, O Lord who could stand?" No one! Most people are convinced that they are accountable to others. Children are accountable to their parents, husbands and wives to each other, workers to their bosses, and bosses to their superiors. We spend much of our time trying to please those to whom we are accountable. One of the great problems of our age is that we have lost our sensitivity toward the One who knows all and who cares about all, and this, of course, is God. Misjudging accountability may need to be developed to some extent in an Easter sermon, especially one that talks about what brought Jesus to the cross and would, if God were only just, seal our fate eternally.

But!

That little word *but* makes all the difference in so many important passages of Scripture. For example, Isaiah writes: *A voice says, "Cry." And I said,*
> *'What shall I cry?" "All men are like grass,*
> *and all their glory is like the flowers of the*
> *field. The grass withers and the flowers fall,*
> *because the breath of the Lord blows on*
> *them. Surely the people are grass. The grass*
> *withers and the flowers fall."*

At this point the prophet is describing the content of any human being's life. It is summed up in having nothing to shout about, no destiny except to be like grass and flowers that fall and dry and blow away. But the prophet's message goes on, and the little word *but* makes all the difference:
> *"The grass withers and the flowers fall, but*
> *the word of our God stands forever."*
> *(Is. 40:6–8)*

The historic Easter psalm, Psalm 118, has this passage in it: "The Lord has chastened me severely, but he has not given me over to death" (Ps. 118:18). In both of these cases, that little word makes all the difference in the world.

In Psalm 130 we also have the little word that makes a difference for eternity. That little word contains the great reversal, which is forgiveness. The Lord takes the ledger and hands it to His Son. It becomes a bitter cup that He grasps in Gethsemane and takes where we deserve to be—to the cross. In our place Jesus is tried and declared to be guilty—not of His sins but of ours, not by the crowd and Pontius Pilate but by the Father. The innocent One bears our punishment in His own body on the cross, and He died there for our sins.

Now God has the ledger in His hands. He grasps it as if to tear it apart from top to bottom, like a curtain in the temple being torn. But we cannot be sure that He has done it, for Jesus lies in the tomb; there is no life and forgiveness if there is no life in Him. Only if He conquers death can we be sure that He has conquered sin and Satan. It is not time yet for the lights to come on and for Easter to begin. We must first wait and hope.

Wait and Hope

The psalmist writes: "I wait for the LORD, my soul waits, and in his word I put my hope. My soul waits for the Lord more than watchmen wait for the morning, more than watchmen wait for the morning" (Ps. 130:5–6). Jürgen Moltmann writes in *Theology of Hope:* "The believer is not set at the high noon of life, but at the dawn of the new day at the point where night and day, things passing and things to come, grapple with each other." Moltmann means that if Christ is not raised, and if the women who went to the tomb found a body and did what they had come prepared to do—to prepare it properly for the sleep of death—then life is over forever. Then *agapē* love, love that reaches to the last and the least deserving, is foolish. Then the grave is the final destination in life, and utter separation from God is the certainty of eternity, and we hope in vain at the death of a loved one or our own death. Then there is no relief from the wars and bloodshed and cruelty that abound in the world, and there is no reason or power to struggle against the way things are. Then the best that we can leave our children is tap-dance lessons, sports abilities, college educations, and our money when we die; there would be nothing more. Then life would be lived as we too often live it—as though Jesus didn't rise from the dead.

But if the tomb is empty when the women arrive, then the things we so foolishly cling to with all our might *are* only passing things. Then the things to come are here now, and life is lived far differently. It is lived in the hope that *agapē* love must and can be lived, that the grave is only a short way station on the way to eternal life, that we must and can call the evil or war and bloodshed what they are—evil and wrong—and never rest until the hope for the peace of God is realized, that there is nothing more important to be shared with our children than the living faith of Easter hope, that life is as new and fresh as the forgiveness of sins, the cleansing of grace, and the power of the risen Christ.

So we approach the tomb with the women at the dawning of a new day, hoping beyond hope, and saying, "I wait for the LORD, my soul waits, and in his word I put my hope" (v. 5).

Hope in the Lord

With the women we approach the tomb. In their hands they carried the spices and ointments. In ours we carry our sins and wrongs, our personal treacheries and tragedies, our hopeless living for ourselves or by the tune that the world pipes for us. Will there be release and cleansing and wholeness here? Is there life after the little deaths and the final death of the tomb?

Then we hear the proclamation from an empty tomb, stone rolled aside:

"He is not here! He is risen!" The sound we heard on Good Friday like the tearing of a curtain separating us from God, like a ledger being torn to pieces in the hands of God, is the sound of grace and forgiveness. He is risen! He conquered sin in His body. He conquered Satan. He conquered even death.

At the open tomb hope dawns—not wishful thinking, not empty dreaming, but living hope in the living Lord. Here is hope that out of every death—the death of divorce, of failure, of lost opportunities—life can be restored; that out of every evil God still is in control, opening up the future for those who trust in Him; that out of every grave of those who die in Christ life eternal will rise.

"O Israel, put your hope in the LORD, for with the LORD there is unfailing love and with Him is full redemption" (v. 7). He has redeemed us by the cross and open tomb. He is risen! We are raised with Him now, and we live in hope that has not and shall not be conquered by any lesser power.

Conclusion

Only at this point can the lights come on, the banners be lifted, the cross unveiled, and the trumpets sound forth. Now the congregation is ready to respond to the announcement "JESUS CHRIST IS RISEN TODAY!" with the words "HE IS RISEN INDEED!"

Sermon Outline

Introduction: The opening words of this psalm could easily have been the sad song of the women who went to the tomb where Jesus had been laid. They were carrying ointments and spices, expecting only to prepare in a less hurried and more thorough manner the body of their dear Master for the sleep of death. Only when we know the hopelessness of life lived in the absence of God, only when we know the deadliness of life without the living God, only when we know the true tragedy of life without the joy of the resurrection will we know how to live in joyous, lively hope.

So we go with the women to the tomb this morning, expecting not the surprise of joy but the gloom of defeat and death and hopelessness. And with them we can then experience

Outline :   Easter: A Time for Renewal of Hope
  I. Renewal of hope can come only out of the depths.
      A. The followers of Jesus had experienced the heights of Jesus' presence.
      B. Their hopes and expectations had been crushed on Good Friday.
      C. Do we live with high hope and high expectation?
  II. Renewal of hope hinges on God's great reversal.
      A. Without the living Christ, we are directly accountable to God.
      B. If God keeps a record of sin, we cannot stand before Him.
      C. Jesus took the ledger of sin to the cross.
      D. But the tomb means failure
  III. Hope waits on God.

A. If Christ is not raised, Jesus' substitutionary death is wasted.
B. If the tomb is empty, hope is fulfilled.
IV. Hope bursts from an empty tomb.
A. The proclamation is given: He is risen!
B. Our sins are cancelled.
C. Hope is focused on God's love and redemption.

Conclusion: Now let the lights come on in your life, and live in the light! Now let the cross be unveiled, for it is a glorious cross of forgiveness! Now let the banners be raised in your life of faith! Now let the lilies of joy trumpet their praise to God: He is risen! Hallelujah! Hope is renewed forever and ever!

LENT
A Time for Renewal

SERMONS

Note: The assignment given the writer of what follows was to develop nine sermons using the Aho/Kapfer material. Quotation marks he had included (indicating *their* content) have been deleted to enhance the flow of the sermons.

The Editors

Ash Wednesday

Lent: A Time for Renewal of Servanthood

Whoever wants to become great among you must be your servant. (Matt. 20:26)

[Here is one approach in using Kapfer's fine material.]

Introduction

What's the strangest bumper sticker you have ever seen? "Let us eschew obfuscation"? "If you like Christians, you'll love Mormons"? "Stamp out bumper stickers"?

Do you have a bumper sticker on your car? Maybe you have the symbol of a fish, the secret recognition sign of the early Christians. But do you know what we all should have? A picture of a towel and a wash basin! Why? Because they are symbols of humility and servanthood.

Of course we wouldn't advertise our humility. But that's what we want to talk about this Ash Wednesday evening. Our emphasis during this Lenten season will be on Lent as a time for the renewal of servanthood. And our specific theme tonight is this: *Although we are often proud and want to lord it over others, Christ calls us to be humble and to be servants of others, as He humbled Himself for us.*

I

It is Maundy Thursday evening. It's a few days after the ugly scene when Mrs. Zebedee came to Jesus and asked that her two sons be given positions of honor by Jesus' side in His kingdom. Now they were all in the Upper Room where the Passover was to be celebrated. Since there were only the Twelve plus Jesus, somebody had to take on the servant's role, for their feet had to be washed before eating. Nobody moved. The food was getting cold. The one who moved would be the doormat, the fool, the loser. The servant would give up his claim to rulership over the others.

Finally, someone *did* move. Jesus took towel and basin, knelt down, and began washing their feet one by one. How could Jesus stoop so low? Then Jesus spoke of the kingdom of the world and the kingdom of heaven. "I have set you an example that you should do as I have done for you. I tell you the truth, no servant is greater than his master, nor is a messenger greater than the one who sent him. Now that you know these things, you will be blessed if you do them" (John 13:15–17).

Is that what happens in your and my life today? A couple sits in the pastor's office, *arms folded,* looking away from each other, saying nothing, for they know that someone has to speak, someone has to give in, and giving in means failure, admission of guilt, humiliation, contempt, and "losing." (Perhaps we need to equip our offices with fewer crosses and more towels and basins. Maybe instead of fish symbols on our doors and crosses on the walls of our homes we need pictures of feet and hands and a towel and basin. It's too bad Albrecht Dürer painted praying hands; maybe wet hands would have been better! And maybe we ought to have drills on how to use towels and basins, much like learning CPR.)

A woman in the altar guild walks into the chancel and sees the flowers neatly arranged by another member of the congregation. She rearranges the flowers the way *she* would like them. *Power. Control.*

A man talks to a few friends and cons them into voting for the person he wants as head of a committee. *Power. Control.* A group of high school students excludes a lonely classmate from their little "in" group. *Power. Control.* A person blessed by God with extra money gives a check to someone who has voluntarily helped the individual in some way. But the gift is not given out of sincere love; the intention is that the person might be indebted to the giver. *Power. Control.*

Are you in any of these pictures? What are the ways in which you and I lack humility and seek to "lord it over" other people? Are you in positions of power? Does power corrupt? The longer you are in a power position, do you think all the more that you deserve it, that there is some great quality within you that others don't have? Or are you a wise steward of your position?

We all may think that our manipulations are only little ways of control, but they can betray a much deeper problem in our hearts—of being *self-serving*, not serving others.

II

Our Lord Jesus Christ gives us quite a different picture of our expected role as Christians. He rejected earthly power both by His words about rulership and by His action of foot washing.

Our Lord Jesus Christ in this Lenten season calls us not just to contemplate His action of humility but to be like Him—little Christs—in all areas of our lives. Think of the power plays we engage in daily as parent over child, spouse to mate, single person with our friends. Think of those where we work whom we would like to control in little ways. Think of fellow Christians in this congregation whom we may try to manipulate so we can have it our way in the things that are planned. Do we really want to serve or to *be* served?

Truly, seeing how far we fall short of being "little Christs," we often need to repent and say with the penitent, "Lord, be merciful to me, a sinner."

III

Lent is a time for renewal. It is a time for a whole new orientation of our hearts. As Peter said to Jesus: "Lord, not just my feet but my hands and my head as well!" (v. 9). We should not sing "Take my life and let it be"—PERIOD! Just "let it be!" But instead, we ask, "Lord, take my life and renew it by the power of your Holy Spirit. Move my whole being not to be served but to serve."

Tonight Servant Jesus bends down from heaven to earth to wash us clean from sin. The One crowned with thorns comes to crown us as children of the kingdom. The naked one comes to place on us the robes of righteousness. The crucified Christ arises from the grave to free us from the world's deadness and to give us a new vision of life and greatness.

Now what does this mean in our daily lives? Are you a parent or a child? God calls you not just out of duty or obligation but in loving response to the Gospel to serve your parents or child because you are in God's kingdom. Are you single? How can you live as a servant with your friends and submit to them? I don't mean that you should be a doormat, but you can serve. You married couples, will you be subject to each other out of reverence for Christ? Members of this congregation, by the power of the Holy Spirit, will you in adoration of our crucified Redeemer make this church a community of care, a haven from selfishness, a place where people serve each other in love?

Servanthood means imitating Jesus, bending down into our lives, kneeling down to serve us, loving us even to His death on the cross.

Servanthood means repenting, being renewed, and learning that "whoever wants to become great among you" must be a servant of Servant Jesus. And the power for this renewal will come to us again and again through our Lord, the great servant who still stoops down to serve us, to cleanse us, to pick us up, and to give us power. We receive His service in our daily searching the Word, in the power of the Holy Spirit affirming our baptism, and in receiving the Lord's Supper with a penitent mind and a joyous heart.

A well-dressed woman from Europe was on safari in Africa. One day she visited a leper colony. There she saw a nurse bending in the dust, tending to the sores of a leper. The heat was intense and the flies were buzzing as she nursed his pus-filled sores. "Why, I wouldn't do that for all the money in the world," said the woman. The nurse quietly replied, "Neither would I."

Are you like that nurse? Our Lord says, "Now that you know these things, you will be blessed if you do them" (v. 17). Oh, may Lent be for you "A Time for Renewal of Servanthood." It begins at the cross. Jesus Himself will hand you the towel and the basin. He will point you to where you should go. Most important, He will go with you. Amen.

Lent: A Time for Renewal of Obedience

Humble yourselves, therefore, under God's mighty hand, that he may lift you up in due time. (1 Peter 5:6)

[Several themes suggest themselves in the material here: pride/humility; obedience; bearing up under suffering; selfless service to others; etc. Here is one tack the preacher may wish to take. (For additional material on humility and obedience see the *Concordia Pulpit* for 1976, pp. 108–13.)]

Introduction

"Life is difficult." Those are the first words in a book that has been widely heralded these last few years: *The Road Less Traveled,* by practicing psychiatrist Dr. M. Scott Peck (New York: Simon and Schuster, 1978). "Life is difficult." And he adds: "This tendency to avoid problems and the emotional suffering inherent in them is *the primary basis of all human mental illness*" (my italics; see the whole paragraph, p. 17).

But in a special dimension, life is particularly difficult for the Christian. God calls us to *total obedience* to *His* design for our lives and regularly *tests* our faithfulness to Him.

A woman was lying on a hospital bed in great pain. As the pastor left, he said cheerily, "Cheer up, God isn't dead!"

"Yeah, I know," she replied, "but I just wish He'd lay off for a little while!"

In our emphasis on the grace and love of God, we sometimes forget that we are to obey God. We are to do what He commands and avoid what He forbids. The Christian life is not only a matter of comforts and thrills, of exciting worship in God's house and unexpected help in trouble. It is also a matter of daily obedience, of humbling ourselves.

In our text Peter equates obeying God with humbling ourselves under God's mighty hand. Peter's words point us to Lent as *a time for renewal of obedience.*

And so our theme for tonight is this: *Although we often proudly resist God's ways and grumble at suffering, He calls us to humility and loving obedience that we might be exalted now and in the life to come.*

I

"Humble yourselves." As the writer to the Hebrews put it: "Consider him who endured such opposition from sinful men, so that you will not grow weary and lose heart" (Heb. 12:3).

Humility! Is it a distinguishing mark of your life? You either have it or you don't. And one can't *work* at being humble either. Remember the classic comment, "Oh, he's very humble. He's got so much to be humble *about!*"

As Paul writes, "Do not think of yourself more highly than you ought, but rather think of yourself with sober judgment, in accordance with the measure of faith God has given you" (Rom. 12:3).

Humility means a quiet recognition of the capacities God has given you balanced by your limitations. It means knowing your shortcomings, but making a full and responsible use of your abilities—to the glory of God.

And this approach to life has to be clearly seen in contrast to the conflicting philosophies that are part of the social fabric of our day. For we live in an age when "competitive supremacy" is the watchword of the day; it has become a major cultural cause of the growth of anxiety among us. And as long as we accept the verdict in our culture that we must be masters in competition, our insecurity will hang on and not be remedied. Instead, Peter says, "humble yourselves." Through God's Word, our Lord speaks straight to our unrelieved anxiety because He is speaking directly to its cause.

As Dr. George Muedeking says (in his excellent study *Emotional Problems and the Bible*), the Scripture here is saying in effect: "Accept the limits ... with which God has endowed you.... God is not interested in success as it is measured by competition. God is concerned that a person's life be developed to the fullness of its potential."

It's like the small fry who comes to Charlie Brown and says, "Yes, sir, Charlie Brown, Abraham Lincoln was a great man. Charlie Brown, would you like to have been Abraham Lincoln?" But he wistfully replies, "Well, I don't know now. I'm having a hard enough time being just plain Charlie Brown!"

As Muedeking notes, God is not interested in success as measured by competition. But God is interested in success as measured by your Spirit-empowered use of your God-given abilities. God is interested that your life be developed to the fullness of its potential. God is concerned that you walk before Him in integrity, that your life be lived honestly and faithfully before Him.

The Son of man came not to be served but to serve and to give His life a ransom for many.

And Christ's spirit is to become yours. You are not here to have God and others serve you. You are here to serve God and to serve the people around you. The question is not, Am I successful? but, How well am I carrying out the tasks of service to others for which God has created me? "We are God's workmanship, created in Christ Jesus to do good works" (Eph. 2:10).

So do you want to overcome the anxiety that flows from a sense of inadequacy in this age of competitive supremacy? Then make this insight your own: *Stop competing with others over whom you have no control.* If you must compete, compete with yourself. And answer the question: Does my record show integrity before God? Remember, it is required in stewards that a person be found *faithful*—not "effective" always, or "successful," but *faithful.* And then go on in faith toward fuller dedication to the service of God in whatever position of life you may be.

So first of all, examine your soul this night and see where you proudly resist God's plan for your life and fail to show true *humility.*

But now consider where you often show your disobedience of God by grumbling at suffering. As Hannah Smith says, "Perfect obedience would be perfect happiness if only we had perfect confidence in the power we were obeying." For God says in effect: "Obedience means turning your back on the problem or the grief and directing your eyes and attention toward Me" (Hannah Smith quoted in Donald L. Deffner, *Bound to Be Free* [Morse Press, 1981], p. 87).

How do you and I learn obedience? By *suffering!* There's a lot of down-to-earth help in 1 Peter for putting suffering into a proper perspective. Consider:

> *It is commendable if a man bears up under the pain of undeserved suffering because he is conscious of God.... If you suffer for doing good and you endure it, this is commendable before God. To this you were called, because Christ suffered for you, leaving you an example, that you should follow in his steps. (1 Peter 2:19–21)*

> *Since Christ suffered in his body, arm yourselves also with the same attitude. (4:1)*

> *Dear friends, do not be surprised at the painful trial you are suffering, as though something strange were happening to you. But rejoice that you participate in the sufferings of Christ, so that you may be overjoyed when his glory is revealed. (vv. 12–13)*

Overjoyed? Can there be *joy* in suffering? I can just guess what you're thinking. That's just too difficult to put into practice! And yet Job in his suffering said, "Though he slay me, yet will I hope in him" (Job 13:15). [See additional illustrations on obedience in submission to God in *The Concordia Pulpit for 1976*, pp. 111–12.]

We need to repent of our lack of trust in God—of our *pride* when we should be *humble,* and of our *grumbling* in suffering when we should see that God is just trying to draw us closer in loving dependence on Him.

II

So obedience and humility before God are often difficult. But obedience to God is possible because God has already exalted us. He has humbled us by His law, of course, so that we recognize our smallness and impurity and His greatness and holiness. But then God exalts us by clothing us with the greatness and the holiness and the life of Jesus Christ. The good news for tonight is that God exalts the humbled. By Jesus' suffering in our place, we have been lifted up, born again to a hope that never dies. We are small and impure, but by God's grace we are the brothers and sisters of the Son of God (Matt. 12:50).

God wants us to humble ourselves—to recognize our unworthiness before Him and to see ourselves as we really are. When we see ourselves as sinners, we will not be so ready to blow our own trumpet or to hear others sing our praises. Recognizing our need for God's grace, we will be in a position to receive it. Relying on that grace, on the gift of God's Son and His Holy Spirit, we are free to search out the good of others, willingly putting on the garment of servanthood.

This humbling, by which we receive God's love and forgiveness and in which we serve those around us, takes place "that [God] may lift you up in due time" (1 Peter 5:6). Even in our struggles and works of service, God enables us to anticipate our final exaltation by giving us an exaltation that is already ours by faith in Christ. We have already been raised with Christ; we have participated in His death and resurrection through our baptism. Our station is an exalted one, but only through Christ and in Christ. Our present exaltation guarantees our future exaltation, which will be greater than anything we can imagine. Our anticipation of the future unfolding of this lifting up, this exaltation, helps us to live in obedience to God as servants to one another, just as Christ was to us.

Because of Jesus, we can truly live in humility—the humility that acknowledges Christ's greatness rather than our own. That greatness Christ showed above all in His willingness to serve us even to the point of death. He was willing to obey His heavenly father because He wanted to save us. Our humility will also express itself in obedience to God and care and service to others. We can expect to suffer here, but God exalts us and will exalt us as He has exalted Christ.

Lent: A Time for Renewal of Witness

Whoever acknowledges me before men, I will also acknowledge him before my Father in heaven. But whoever disowns me before men, I will disown him before my Father in heaven. (Matt. 10:32–33)

Introduction

Several students were walking across the quadrangle of a large university just as the bell tower chimed five o'clock in the afternoon. At that precise moment a foreign student on the sidewalk in front of them dropped full length on the ground to the utter amazement of those walking behind him. After the initial shock the students realized that he had not stumbled or fallen but was a Muslim prostrating himself at his holy hour of prayer.

That man was not ashamed of his religion. How many of us are not ashamed to make known that we are Christians? How many of us, by omitting prayer or other practices that might designate that we are Christians, in effect become guilty of sinning as Peter did when he said, "I don't know the man!" (Matt. 26:74)? What a tragedy for those who have been nominal members of the church but about whom Christ will one day say, "I never knew you" (7:23)! [From Donald Deffner, *Bold Ones on Campus* (CPH, 1973), p. 63.]

That's what we're going to address this evening in our Lenten series: "Lent: A Time for Renewal." It is also a time for renewal of *witness*.

And our theme is this: *Although we may often feel inadequate in our witnessing or fear others' opinions of us, Christ frees us from fear and empowers us to a bold commitment in word and deed.*

I

The words of our text are pretty clear, aren't they? Deny Christ in your life with explicit rejection of him as Peter did, and Christ will say on the Last Day, "I never knew you!" Or deny Christ by joining the secret service, like people at the end of the gospel of Mark ("They said nothing to anyone, because they were afraid"—16:8), and keep a zipper on your lip about your faith, and on the Last Day Christ will say, "I have nothing to say for you, either!"

In Jerusalem in certain temples the incense is very heavy. As pilgrims return to their homes or meet friends on the street, other people can tell where they have been.

Can other people tell where you have been, where you are coming from, and where you are going? Have your eyes "seen the King"?

Remember the story of the prodigal son. The "distant country" in that story is any condition *in your own life*—wherever you are—that keeps you away from God. What "distant country" may you be in right now? What have you placed in your life *before* God that keeps you from a faithful witness to Him?

A milk-truck driver came to a campus pastor and told him of a student attending his chapel who lived with the driver in his boarding house. Because of the example of that student's faith the man wanted to join the Lutheran church. "That man has a faith to live by," he said. "I want that faith."

Could people say that about you?

When we examine ourselves (1 Cor. 11:28), we must admit that we are often like Peter. We live as if to say, "I don't know the man." We need to repent.

Gerhard Aho has noted that we cannot confess Jesus Christ before the world unless at the same time we ask God's forgiveness for our own sin and are grateful for having experienced God's goodness and mercy. Confession of sin, praise of Christ, and witness to His Gospel in word and deed before the world belong together inseparably. Where one of these is missing, the confession is falsified.

II

Although we may feel inadequate in our witnessing or fear others' opinions of us, Christ frees us from fear and empowers us to a bold commitment in word and deed.

Many sermons and their hearers never get beyond talking *about* the need to evangelize, and people nod their heads and say, "Yeah, I should witness more." Then they go home *and nothing happens.*

Where is the logjam here? We are not saying that each of you needs to go up and down the streets of our city and ring the doorbells of strangers' homes like the Mormons and Jehovah's Witnesses. (Although there *is* a time for the *right* kind of evangelization canvassing.) We are not saying that you have to be a "professional" witness or be like those who are gifted in expressing themselves.

But we are saying that you can be what you are—a baptized, redeemed child of God—and tell people who your real Father is.

And you can let your Christian walk *show far more in the natural relationships* of your daily life.

Be what you are! A woman came up to a pastor after an evangelization presentation and said, "In that whole hour, there's one thing you said which I liked the most."

"What is that?" asked the pastor.

"That though some of us may fumble or stumble in our witness, we should still speak up for Christ. Fumbling . . . stumbling . . . that's me," she said.

Often our witness is far more powerful than that of the person with the clerical collar because it is not from a "professional." Every one of us can say in our own "fumbling, stumbling" way, "This is what Jesus means to me."

So let your faith show *naturally* in your everyday life.

In *Why People Join the Church* (Pilgrim, 1980), Edward A. Rauff lists the reasons people "drop back in" to the church: the influence of Christian people; family relationships and responsibilities; the search for community; a personal crisis; a feeling of emptiness; the end of rebellion; the journey toward truth; the response to evangelism; the reaction to guilt and fear; God's *kairos* (a fitting time); a church visit, program, special event, or sacred act; and the influence of pastors.

But of all these, friends or relatives were the most frequent source of evangelization.

As Gerhard Knutson of St. James Lutheran Church in Crystal, Minnesota, has said:

> *The resource is the living rooms and kitchens of the homes of the congregation. The most beautiful and natural place for the gospel is ordinary folk in honest communication in their homes talking and listening to one another about what really matters in life. . . . To become equal, to divest myself of any "expert" status, I come not to get or want anything but to understand and to care. (Gerhard Knutson, "Listening Witness," an outline of procedures for evangelism at St. James Lutheran Church, Crystal, Minnesota. Mimeographed paper distributed through ALC Evangelical Outreach training events, 1978, p. 3.)*

And in so sharing our faith in the natural setting of our workplace and home, we are not to fear. Even when persons may ridicule us, Christ's promise is there: "When they arrest you, do not worry about what to say or how to say it. At that time you will be given what to say, for it will not be you speaking, but the Spirit of your Father speaking through you" (Matt. 10:19–20).

So we rely on His Gospel promise to remove our fear and renew our witness.

The power is in the Gospel, not in ourselves. And that power does come to us when we faithfully use the means of grace, the Word and the sacraments. They are the power supply for our witness to our Savior and His death and resurrection for us.

Dr. Howard Kelly, famed surgeon of Baltimore and renowned for the Christian principles he maintained in his profession, was seldom seen without a beautiful rosebud in the lapel of his coat. It remained fresh for a long time, and there was a reason. When people asked him the secret, he turned the lapel and showed them a little glass vial containing water. The stem of the rose went through the buttonhole into the water and thus kept fresh for a longer time. Dr. Kelly would then tell inquirers that the secret of beautiful and fragrant Christian living lies in drawing refreshment from the water of life, Jesus Christ (Wilbur E. Nelson, *Anecdotes and Illustrations* [Baker, 1971], p. 44.)

That water of life is yours now (and always has been) in your baptism (Rom. 6:3–4). Now tell others about that living water. As Isaiah says, "Come, all you who are thirsty, come to the waters; and you who have no money, come, buy and eat! Come, buy wine and milk without money and without cost" (Is. 55:1).

So will your life be different this week? Listen to how one businessman put it:

> *Jesus, I need You to remind me that even though I'm part of management, I still belong to a union: the brotherhood of Christ . . . I need You to remind me that competitors, fellow employees, suppliers, and customers are people You love as much as You love me and that I am supposed to do likewise. Show me (for I am blind) the many opportunities I have each day to let people see You through me. . . .*
>
> *Lord, I also thank You. I thank you for granting me whatever talent I have for the business I'm in . . . and for enjoying my work. Remind me to treat it as sacred, as a vocation, as a means to fulfill my Christian commitment . . . not as a separate island of my life. Most of all, Lord, remind me that I am* baptized . . . not "was" baptized . . . *every minute of every day, especially from nine to five.* (Wally Armbruster, *It's Still Lion v. Christian in the Corporate Arena* (CPH, 1979), p. 117)

Lord, "Thee I love with all my heart." Amen.

Lent: A Time for Renewal of True Religion

They tie up heavy loads and put them on men's shoulders,
but they themselves are not willing to lift a finger to move
them. (Matt. 23:4)

[In this sermon I have pointedly quoted much of Kapfer's rich material, again laying out one approach to the theme, adding a vignette or two of my own.]

Introduction

You may all have heard the response to the comment, "There are too many hypocrites in the church; that's why I haven't joined."

The reply: "Come on in! There's always room for one more!"

The message tonight will make us all squirm just a little—or perhaps a great deal! The opposite of true religion is false religion, and who among us isn't guilty of a little playacting about our religion, especially in living out our religion? Who among us doesn't have a public face and a private face, a spiritual "sitting room" where the real person sits—warts and all!

Will the real "you" please stand up?

And this is our theme tonight: *Although we can be phonies (in our religious life) and not practice what we preach, God calls us to practice true religion and to say, "I'm not good; I'm forgiven!"*

I

In our text Jesus is speaking of the Pharisees who proudly called attention to their works but actually were self-indulgent and loveless toward others (Matt. 23:13–14, 25–36). In a nutshell, they did not practice what they preached (v. 3).

Nobody likes a phony. Perhaps we are better at spotting phoniness in others than we are in ourselves. Phonies are people who make sure that their name is on the letterhead of civic and charitable organizations but don't lift a hand to do any work. Phonies take courses in listening skills and sensitivity training, but they use their training to manipulate people rather than to help them. The insincerity of a phony is eventually spotted. The phony likes to use people. The phony is a pretender.

Are you ever a phony?

The worst phony is the phony Christian, for false, phony, hypocritical Christians can hurt the faith of others, and they eventually come to believe their own lies.

Phony religion led to the excesses of the Middle Ages and the Spanish Inquisition. Phony religion made the Reformation necessary. It is phony religion that is preached and proclaimed so often by some radio and television preachers. (What they need is a new magazine titled *Repenthouse.*)

Phony religion is evident when a church like one in Kentucky proclaims: "We are seven miles from any known form of sin."

Religious fanatics believe that they alone have the truth and that everyone else is the enemy.

The Passion account (in the Gospel tonight) focuses on Jesus and His confrontation with Caiaphas. Jesus represents true religion; Caiaphas represents false religion that has gotten out of hand.

Caiaphas was a Pharisee. The Pharisees followed 613 rules that interpreted the commands of God; they actually kept those rules and insisted that others do the same. For them, religion was not a matter of the heart responding to God's love; it was a matter of keeping cold rules and regulations. Those rules left no room for penitent, weak believers.

Phony religion (like that of Caiaphas) happens when "goodness" becomes the central mark of the Christian life. If one is good, one is a believer. If one is not good, one is not a believer. The church is composed of only good people. No one else may apply. In a wealthy parish in a suburb of St. Louis a voting member once proposed that membership be by invitation only. Happily, the resolution did not pass.

Jesus came to seek and save all people. He spoke about the 99 and the one. If goodness is the mark, one of two things happens. We either become phonies and hypocrites, or we are led to despair. That is, if we must be good, we will try to keep outwardly whatever rules need to be kept in order to be considered good. Inevitably, one day we will either get weary of living rigidly under the rules (many children do, and as a result, they rebel), or we will cover up every bad thing we do. Then we will be quick to condemn others. We will have absolutely no word of hope for those who don't keep the rules, for there is no hope.

On the other hand, we may not try to cover up, but the result will be just as tragic. We will have nowhere to go, for if only good people can be accepted by a good God and His good followers, we will despair of any hope.

II

Jesus broke through the goodness trap and insisted that the mark of the believer is not goodness. It is forgiveness. While the Pharisees and scribes whispered, "This man receives sinners," the sinners rejoiced to say, "This man receives sinners and eats with them." Lost sheep know that they have strayed, have not been good, and would be lost forever had the Good Shepherd not come, gone to the bramble bush of the cross, taken their badness on Himself, and died. Out of an open tomb He comes, shouting for all to hear: "Look who I found! Rejoice with me!" He is carrying you and me!

The renewal of true religion happens when we confess that the religion of our goodness is false. It gets in the way of the Good Shepherd. True religion happens when we know and believe that we lost sheep have been found; that's what the Christian faith is all about. We have a Savior who receives sinners and communes with them, who lives in them, who changes their hearts into hearts of love so that they are able to say with gladness and joy, "There's hope for others, for look at what God has done and is still doing with someone like me."

Can you see in your life where phony religion can be overcome by the true religion that comes from the cross?

True religion happens when we make sure that our lives point to Jesus, who receives sinners and eats with them. We say, "Look at me. I'm not good; I am forgiven!" One Christian even had this bumper sticker on her car: CHRISTIANS AREN'T PERFECT—JUST FORGIVEN. We need to say that to those who have wronged us so that they may know of another way to live. We need to say this to our children so that they are not burdened with the guilt of not being good but are free in the joy of being forgiven sinners like us. We need to say that in our churches so that no one fails to enter them because they feel unworthy and that no one who enters our churches leaves without knowing that Jesus receives them and offers His love and forgiveness to them.

A pastor once passed through the narthex and, unknown to his secretary, overheard her talking to a stranger sitting in the back pew.

"May I help you?" asked the secretary. "No," said the woman. "I only came into this church to pray. I'm not really a member anywhere."

"Well," said the secretary, "I want you to know that whatever burdens you have, you need not bear them alone. Our people will help you bear your cross" (From Donald L. Deffner, *Here, Take My Hand*).

Yes, Jesus receives sinners. His goodness becomes ours. Goodness is not wrong, of course. We ought to be good, for goodness is a fruit of the Spirit. But goodness is not our chief mark. Faith in Jesus Christ, who forgives our sins—our lack of goodness—is our chief mark. Caiaphas declared Jesus "not good," "guilty." Yet that was God's plan—that the innocent Jesus, good in every way, be declared guilty so that He might take our guilt on Himself to the cross and crucify our guilt to death in His body. We live by faith in Christ, who is our substitute and the source of all goodness.

Faith is not static. It is not faith in a set of religious propositions behind which we can conveniently hide. Faith is a loving relationship that trusts in God's mercy and responds in godly actions. To proclaim that Christian education is important without growing in it and making sure that our Sunday school children grow in it is phony. To say that we have an important mission and ministry as Christ's church without supporting that mission with our time, talent, and treasure is phony. To say that Christ has called us to demonstrate our faith through acts of loving service to the world around us without acting on that belief is phony. It is to be religious without true religion, who is Jesus, standing before us, wanting to put His nail-marked hands into the bramble bush where we have strayed.

What a terrible thing phony religion is! It is essentially living a lie not just before people but, most tragically, before God. That was the tragedy of Caiaphas. That is the tragedy that can befall us if we live the lie that we are good, for then we wouldn't need God. But we do need God, for we are not good. God knows that. He gave us Jesus. Regardless of the bramble bush of guilt, self-protection, or a judgmental nature in which you may live, let go with a shout: "Here I am hiding, guilty and helpless. Reach for me, God!" He will! He has—in Jesus. And He will put you on His shoulder rejoicing—and you also will rejoice!

Lent 5

Lent: A Time for Renewal of Priorities

Do not love the world or anything in the world. If anyone loves the world, the love of the Father is not in him. For everything in the world—the cravings of sinful man, the lust of his eyes and the boasting of what he has and does—comes not from the Father but from the world. The world and its desires pass away, but the man who does the will of God lives forever. (1 John 2:15–17)

[This introductory note is written in Thessalonica during a Concordia Theological Seminary, Fort Wayne-sponsored tour, "In the Footsteps of St. Paul." How brother Aho, now "with the Lord," would have enjoyed this trip with some of his colleagues and students! And in his comments on this text how aptly he catches the contrast between the pagan spirit of this world and that of the kingdom of God! We also saw a modern, secular Thessalonica not unlike the one Paul confronted two millennia ago. The apostle John addresses his "dear children" in that type of pagan setting.]

Introduction

Imagine that you are at a thrilling football or basketball game. The atmosphere is tense. The score is tied. The outcome is critical. Your team has the ball. You can hear the roar as the crowd yells: "GO! GO! GO! GO!"

Now imagine another scene. The apostle John is sitting in a hut on the edge of the Mediterranean Sea, dictating a letter that will be sent to his people around Ephesus. He looks out at the beautiful white clouds scudding like ocean liners above the azure sea. Then he hears the distant roar of the crowds at the games in the area. He tells his scribe to write: "Do not love the world or anything in the world. If anyone loves the world, the love of the Father is not in him. For everything in the world—the cravings of sinful man, the lust of his eyes and the boasting of what he has and does—comes not from the Father but from the world. The world and its desires pass away, but the man who does the will of God lives forever" (1 John 2:15–17).

These words of John are not just remote sayings from the distant past. They have relevance for our lives here tonight. And in the next few minutes we shall see: *Though we may be enticed to crave the world's pleasures (and its false teachings), Christ empowers us to resist and remain His faithful children.*

I

In the first part of his letter, John discusses the life of fellowship with God that is demonstrated by love for fellow believers and lack of love for the world. Those who know God as their Father and Christ as their Redeemer are ready to heed the warning, "Do not love the world." As the Phillips translation says it:

> Never give your hearts to this world or to any of the things in it. A man cannot love the Father and love the world at the same time. For the whole world-system, based as it is on men's desires, their greedy ambitions and the glamour of all that they think splendid, is not derived from the Father at all, but from the world itself. The world and all its passionate desires will one day disappear. But the man who is following God's will is part of the permanent and cannot die.

Lent is a time for renewal of priorities. How can we avoid letting love for the world take priority over love for our heavenly Father?

Don't get me wrong here. In telling us not to love the "world," John doesn't mean we have to give up the good gifts God has given us to enjoy in His good creation. He is not condemning material things in and of *themselves*. This evening I *affirm* such good gifts of God as a nice home, new clothes, a colorful jogging suit, steak (prepared any way you like it), a new car, a good glass of beer, a really neat necktie, a lovely cashmere sweater, new camera equipment, and so on.

We *affirm* all these good gifts from God to us. But we can fall in *love* with these things. We can become coddled with creature comforts and live like people of the world who are filled with a false piety, pep pills, and popular psychology. We can follow the pattern of this world and become part of the mass in our culture that lives *primarily* for material things. We can become *submerged* in our culture and become just part of the pasteurized mass. We can become "the bland being led by the bland."

But the life of the falsely secure person is not all bliss. Burt E. Coody describes the vague image one can have of the "mental, imaginary house of security" one lives in. Is it like yours?

"In it are the rooms of the organization, the vocation, the job. Does your job, your work, have first claim over your soul? Or does God have first claim?"

There is the family room—anything for the kids these days! "There is the living room for entertainment and social status." There is the "den for comfort, relaxation, sports, the bedroom for sleep. . . ." But "the foundation for this whole structure is *money and social status* provided by being a member of the 'in group.' When these are removed the whole structure falls, and (one) is plunged either into despair or defiance" (*The Pulpit* [July 1958], p. 20).

But while it's still going, and the "mental imaginary house of security" has not crumbled and fallen, it's a pretty good life.

You don't need people any more as long as you have machines, computers, *things. You don't need God anymore.*

A campus pastor tells of a visit with a young woman at the University of California in Berkeley:

> *She was a brilliant student from Chile, lived*
> *at International House, and had visited our*
> *University Lutheran Chapel with friends.*
> *When I called on her, she explained that she*
> *had tried to find God all her life, but with-*
> *out success. "Every night for nine years I*
> *read my Spanish Bible," she told me, "and*
> *prayed for faith. But God never gave it to*
> *me."*
> *We talked some more, and finally I quietly*
> *asked, "Did you ever pray for forgiveness?"*
> *She was silent.*
> *Then, as we talked, she commented that she*
> *had never broken any of the Ten Command-*
> *ments. Intrigued, and not having approached*
> *anyone this way before, I went through the*
> *commandments with her, starting, however,*
> *with the last. No, she had never coveted. No,*
> *she had never stolen, No, she had never had*
> *an adulterous thought. No, she had never*
> *sworn, etc. Finally we got to the first com-*
> *mandment. "Is there anything—anything at*
> *all," I asked, "that you would place before*
> *giving yourself wholly up to God?"*
> *She paused wistfully. "I will have to say . . ."*
> *and then she spoke firmly, "if anything—*
> *anything—would come in the way of my*
> *pursuing my diplomatic career, it would*
> *have to go."*
> For whoever keeps the whole law and yet
> stumbles at just one point is guilty of breaking
> all of it" *(James 2:10).*
> *The tragedy in this instance was that this dy-*
> *namic young woman was gradually going*
> *blind. But her real blindness was in not*
> *seeing the Savior, who wanted to reach out*
> *and give her faith, but only as she received—*
> *having sought—forgiveness. (Bound to Be*
> Free, p. 135)

Is there any area in your life—any area at all—in which you place God second? John warns us not to give our hearts to "the cravings of sinful man, the lust of his eyes and *the boasting of what he has and does."*

In sum, God, through the apostle John, is making clear how Christians are to relate to the sinful world around them.

We know the changeless, eternal Christ, who redeemed us. Why should we wish to conform to a changing, evil world that is passing away? We know the Father and His great love for us, by which we have become His children. Why should we fall in love with the world, which will leave us only with remorse and hopelessness? Furthermore, by the power of God's Word abiding in us we have, in Christ, already overcome the prince of this world (1 John 2:14). We have within us the power to resist the world's enticements, the power not to give in to its evil ways. Our life is rooted ultimately in our relationship with the God of love. Out of that relationship flows our proper relating to the evil world. We cannot love the world, not when that love would lead us away from the God of love.

The trouble is, you and I often fail. We need to repent. And so tonight again we say: "Lord, be merciful to me, a sinner."

II

In this Lenten service our suffering Savior calls you and me again not to let love for the world take priority in our life over love for the Father.

We have been moved by the Spirit to do God's will by believing His love for us.

God demonstrated His love for us in Christ's suffering and death.

God demonstrated His love for us by giving us, in our baptism, faith in the Christ who made us the priority of His life.

God demonstrates His love for us by not letting us perish with the world but by keeping us forever with Him.

We now continue to do God's will by loving Him.

We can love God rather than the evil world because God has enabled us to say: "For to me, to live is Christ and to die is gain" (Phil. 1:21).

Are you like that faithful Christian college student who every night before going to bed drew aside the curtain at his window and said, "Perhaps tonight, Lord?" And every morning on arising he would draw aside the curtain, look up to the heavens, and say, "Perhaps today, Lord?"

We can love God rather than the evil world because we have been crucified with Christ; it is no longer we who live but Christ who lives in us, and the life we now live in the flesh we live by faith in the Son of God, who loved us and gave Himself for us (Gal. 2:20).

And you and I—in Christ—shall live forever!

Lent: A Time for Renewal of Godly Fear

You did not receive a spirit that makes you a slave again to fear, but you received the Spirit of sonship. (Rom. 5:15)

Introduction

Imagine that you walked into church tonight, and instead of the cross above the altar, you saw a hangman's noose. Or imagine you saw an electric chair bolted high on the chancel wall. What would you think? "Who put *that* there? What kind of a prank *is* this?"

And yet the cross is the heart of our faith. And we shouldn't think of it as looking like the one seen in a bookstore window with the sign: "This beautiful gilded crucifix on easy terms." The cross did not come with "easy terms." It cost Christ His life—for us.

The cross is a strange place to look for *renewal.* Renewal implies a new beginning. Calvary signals an ending. Renewal implies hope, new possibilities, and new ways of living. Yet if there is hope for renewal here, there is hope for renewal anywhere. *If there is hope for renewal in a dying thief, there is hope for renewal of anyone—including you and me.*

There is hope for you here in this church tonight. No matter what you may have done in your life, there is hope and forgiveness here. We need to learn how to pray the prayer of our brother, the publican: "God, be merciful to me, a sinner." And tonight we pray the prayer of our brother, the thief: "Jesus, remember me."

I

First, let's consider when terror—fear—is appropriate.

To fear God is not always bad. The dying thief on the cross first needed to feel fear of God—terror toward God. He knew then what he had spent his life avoiding: Life is lived in the presence of God. It doesn't matter that the world—our friends, family, co-workers—says that something is right or wrong, good or bad. *God alone matters.* When we realize at a moment of decision that we are in God's presence and that our choice will show either that we love God or that we love the world or ourselves, that is *good* fear. It is godly fear. It is the only voice that our sinful desires will hear. How many times haven't we needed to say, "I cannot do this, for God is present. I cannot sin against the high and holy God!" That's fear, and it's *good* fear.

Perhaps one of the reasons people make and break marriage vows so casually is that there is no fear of God in them. The same can be said of the many lifestyles that lead nowhere except away from God. How many people have a casual religion about a God whose presence can be taken casually?

Perhaps another reason the fear of God isn't present in so many is because we have succumbed to pop psychology—*removing guilt without confessing it,* which is merely a cover-up.

A popular book a few years ago was titled *I'm OK, You're OK.* It should have been titled *You're Not OK, I'm Not OK—and That's OK* because of the forgiveness of our sins in Jesus Christ.

Or maybe fear of God is missing because we moralize in our life, thinking that Christianity is heavy doses of shoulds and shouldn'ts. We think that Christianity is "keeping the Ten Commandments"—but we *cannot* keep them. We fail utterly and must look to Christ alone, who kept the Law perfectly in our stead. And He alone now gives us, as forgiven and newly empowered people, the grace to let the "fruit of the Spirit" show forth in our lives.

Perhaps the proper fear of God is missing because people avoid listening to the "still, small voice" that hovers near if we only face up to our personal, apart-from-everything-and-everyone-else confrontation with God.

All of these reasons fell away for the thief, as they will for us, when death—that completely personal experience—is faced. But we can't wait until then. For us and our congregation, this Lent is "A Time for Renewal of Godly Fear." Part of that renewal must involve *taking another look at the cross.* We need to recognize the presence of God through the assimilation in our daily lives of true, honest, and complete Law and of lavish and wondrous grace.

But fear is not enough. The thief was filled with godly fear—fear of God. But he needed more than fear, for in that fear he would soon die forever.

II

Now let's look at fear as slavery.

Fear is not to be our master that takes us captive and keeps us there. Much of the resentment against legalistic religion (one that is mostly "rules and regulations") is well founded, for it operates with fear as its motivation. When fear of God remains only terrified fear, then guilt, failure, and sin are never removed, and either consciences die or people break free and enter another slavery—living without the proper fear of God.

A pastor tells of a woman, the happy and efficient wife of a fellow pastor, who was experiencing her full share of life's sunshine and shade, but no real darkness filled her way. Then without warning her husband died of a heart attack, leaving her terribly alone and afraid—afraid of her own decisions, afraid of the present, afraid of the future. When the pastor visited his colleague's wife, he found her in the vicelike grip of fear, so tyrannized that most of her time was spent in bed. She was so terrified that she became bedridden.

When the pastor saw her two years later, he was pleasantly surprised to find a poised, serene woman, working as a receptionist in an insurance office. When the pastor asked her to explain her amazing recovery, the woman replied, "The work helped, of course, but I couldn't work at all until I faced my fear and saw it was basically a selfish rebellion against God and what I thought was God's will. When I saw that, I began to pray that God would forgive my selfishness. And as I prayed, I became aware of God's hand reaching down to me, and the Holy Spirit moved me to reach up in faith until I finally clasped that hand. And then to my amazement, I found His hand clasping mine, and I knew that He really cared and that He would help me as long as I held His hand in faith" (From Donald L. Deffner, *Sermon Illustrations for the Gospel Lessons* [CPH, 1980], p. 25).

III

Let's consider *fear conquered.*

At first the thief tried to transfer his fear to Jesus by reviling Him. Now in the grand reversal of that transference, hope dawned. If this man [Jesus] is innocent and yet is dying, the thief may have thought, and if I am guilty and am dying, I know why *I* am here. But why is *He* here? Could God be here in my fear, my guilt, and my death? Could God be here in order that my shame and guilt might indeed be transferred to Him? But how? The thief couldn't get off the cross and place his life on Jesus' cross. He was nailed down and dying. He was helpless to act. He could not save himself. He could do only one thing. He could say, "Jesus, remember me when you come into your kingdom" (Luke 23:42). Remember *me!* Not my sins and guilt. Remember *me!* Be here for *me!* Suffer here for *me!* Die here for *me!* Let your kingdom claim *me!*

Are those also our words tonight? Then the promise comes to us, as it came to him: "I tell you the truth, today you will be with me in paradise" (v. 43). The load of sin is lifted. The guilt is gone. The fear was also gone. Now he could soon enter the presence of God, with only this on his lips: "I am guilty. I am not worthy to be called Your child. But Jesus died for me. He gave to me the promise of paradise."

Soon he would hear the voice of the Father: "I know you. You are mine. Come, O blessed one. Enter the place prepared for you from eternity."

And God says that to you tonight, no matter who you are or what you have done. "I know you. You are mine. Come, O blessed one. Enter the place prepared for you from eternity."

The thief is *not* the exception. The thief is the rule by which you and I live and die and live eternally—the rule of grace and mercy by faith in Jesus Christ.

IV

Finally, let us look at "fear" as awe of God, as sanctified reverence.

How will you spend the rest of your life? The thief spent what little time he had left in his life—perhaps four or five hours before the soldiers came to break his legs and speed up his death—living in a new kind of godly fear. It is called the godly *reverence,* the *awe* of living in the Lord's presence. *The cross became an altar of praise.*

Jesus promised the kingdom to the thief, and he learned *godly* fear, the *awe* of God. That's the other side of godly fear—to know and believe that we live in the presence of God and His kingdom now and for eternity.

That's the gift of paradise. Paradise is not something we claim only at the end of our lives. It claims us *now. Paradise* opens when we commune at the Lord's Table, for there God focuses His presence because Christ is there. *Paradise* opens when we realize that God is present to be reverenced in the decisions we make, in the people we serve, in the work we do, in the friends we love, in the families where He has placed us. Paradise *now* is not heavenly bliss. That will come in God's good time later. Paradise *now* is the realization that we live in the Lord's presence at all times and in every circumstance, that where we are, God's holy name is present to be reverenced, obeyed, and celebrated.

Godly fear (true *awe* of our great and wonderful God) is the heart of the faithful one—you!—exclaiming with joy: "Lord, you remembered me! Help *me* to remember *You!*"

Lent: A Time for Renewal of Christian Unity

Is not the cup of thanksgiving for which we give thanks a participation in the blood of Christ? And is not the bread that we break a participation in the body of Christ? Because there is one loaf, we, who are many, are one body, for we all partake of the one loaf. (1 Cor. 10:16–17)

[In this sermon I not only wanted to stress the unity/corporate nature of Holy Communion but also the individual *need* of the Christian to commune more frequently. The word "participation" is used twice in the text.]

Introduction

I read once of a family that practiced forgiveness around their fireplace each New Year's Eve. They would take down the last year's calendar from the wall, and a page at a time they would remember the events of the past year.

January would be torn off first, and with it came memories of a birthday party or some other joyous family event. After a laugh or a "Remember that?" January would be laid in the flames. This would be done 11 more times, until the last month's page was put in the fire.

But not all the memories were happy ones. There were times the family members could recall the anger, the misunderstandings, the hurt and pain they had caused each other. But they also recalled the *forgiveness* that Christ had made possible between them and that they had shared with each other.

That's the kind of forgiveness to practice—daily to be sure, but also forgiveness for all the sins and failures of the past as God has forgiven us: totally.

That's the forgiveness of which we are assured in the Holy Eucharist. Our sins are forgiven, indeed *have been* forgiven in the once-for-all act of Jesus' death on Calvary and His resurrection on Easter morn.

Note the words in our text for tonight. *Participation* is stressed twice: "Is not the cup of thanksgiving for which we give thanks a *participation* in the blood of Christ? Is not the bread that we break a *participation* in the body of Christ?" And so we *come often* to the Lord's Supper.

And what joy is ours tonight! Observe the atmosphere in the chancel. The note of sorrow that we have heard all Lent is stilled this evening, and the Holy Supper is celebrated with rejoicing. The mood is one of exultation, not gloom.

What is really happening here?

I

Holy Communion is not a dead doctrine but a dynamic drama. It is stirring, moving. It has a cast of characters: God and humanity. The script for the drama is in the Holy Scriptures. The plot is almost melodramatic: It is the rescue of a fallen child through an amazing plan devised by the divine Father. And this drama is told every time we celebrate Holy Communion.

We are swept with all humanity into the gripping plot as it develops. Here each week, as we take our place in the wings of the stage of history and witness the drama of the Lord's institution of His Holy Supper, we see the broad sweep of the dramatic events of salvation pass before our eyes again as we remember the Lord's death until He comes again.

At least that is what this service of joy and praise is *supposed* to be. But how often is it that way for you?

Did you ever attend Holy Communion in a church where the service was less a thanksgiving than a test of faith? The Gloria in Excelsis was sung like a funeral dirge. There was no joy of sins forgiven, no lifting up of hearts. The service was not a Te Deum ("We praise You, O God") but *tedium!* How can one expect to be spiritually refreshed when a congregation has lost the concept of joyful thanks that the Lord meant for us to share in the Blessed Sacrament of His body and blood? Some people have still not grasped the meaning and blessings of the Lord's Supper.

As Berthold von Schenck once wrote:

> *Doubtless this is the cause of much spiritual weakness in our church life. It was not so in the beginning. The central worship of the early Church was the Holy Communion. The prime motive which led Christians to form themselves into a fellowship was the desire to worship in their special Christian way. That was the celebration of the Holy Communion. Back of their coming together was, first and foremost, the desire to celebrate the Real Presence of Christ in the Communion. We have gone a far way from the pristine Church.* (*The Presence: An Approach to the Holy Communion* [New York: Ernst Kaufmann, 1945], pp. 23–24)

Or as another author puts it:

> *This realization of the death of our Lord is a means of an* active fellowship with Christ. *The believer absolutely yields his person to that transcendent vision of his crucified Redeemer, and thus enters into communion with Christ himself. Christ takes him, penetrates him, and "assimilates him to himself."* (Olin Alfred Curtis, *The Christian Faith* [New York: Eaton & Mains, 1905], pp. 432–33)

Do you sense this closeness with Christ as you commune? Do you *forget yourself, your* record of performing during the week, *your* deeds, *your* offerings to God, and instead, *at this altar,* open yourself up to Him and say, "Here, Lord, I am empty; fill me with yourself!"

> *Nothing in my hand I bring;*
> *Simply to thy cross I cling.*
> *Naked, come to thee for dress;*
> *Helpless, look to thee for grace;*
> *Foul, I to the fountain fly;*
> *Wash me, Savior, or I die.*
>
> (*Lutheran Worship* 361:3)

Are those *your* words?

One of the saddest, most misinformed views of the Sacrament is from the person who says, "I don't go to the Lord's Supper unless I've really been improving in my spiritual life, unless I've really cleaned up the things I've done wrong and have really become *worthy* of going to communion."

What a perversion of the meaning of the Sacrament! It may come from a misunderstanding of the words in the King James Version: "He that eateth and drinketh *unworthily,* eateth and drinketh damnation to himself" (1 Cor. 11:29).

But those words do not mean that you can become "worthy" to go to the Lord's Supper. *None of us can.* Our "worthiness" can only come from Christ, who gives us the forgiveness of our sins. The words *really* mean that whoever eats and drinks without being *penitent,* without being *sorry* for one's sins, eats and drinks judgment on oneself.

The Lord's Supper is not for the *righteous* person but for the sinner— *and that means everybody in this church tonight!*

So it's not what you and I bring to God. Our hands are empty. It's *God giving us of Himself.* He gives us the body and the blood of His Son for the forgiveness of our sins.

So let us *participate*—as our text stresses twice.

But then Paul goes on to point out: "Because there is one loaf, we, who are many, are one body, for we all partake of the one loaf."

II

At the same time that we note the intensely *personal* nature of the Lord's Supper, we also need to grasp the powerful *corporate* experience involved.

Maundy Thursday is a *time for renewal of Christian unity.* It is a renewal in our common Lord, our common blessings, and our common task.

It is a time for renewal in our common Lord so that we can be done with those things that usurp Christ's place within our hearts.

It is a time for renewal in our common blessings so that the life of Jesus may be manifested in our mortal bodies (2 Cor. 4:10–11).

It is a time for renewal in our common task of confessing our faith, making a unanimous confession of all that Christ has taught (Matt. 28:20).

It is a time to share our joys and sorrows (1 Cor. 12:26).

It is a time to stand together against Satan. We will not be such easy prey for Satan when we remain in fellowship with each other. We can better resist Satan when we strengthen our fellowship by partaking of Holy Communion (Acts 2:42).

We are not solo Christians. We need each other. Alone, we stumble and fall. United in Christ, we move ahead, empowered by the Holy Spirit to do His will.

You and I, members of _____ Church, are we united in the work our Lord has given us to do? Our Lord strengthens our unity again in Holy Communion here tonight. It is a time for renewal of our Christian unity in a common Lord, common blessings, and a common task. Then we will be a body of Christians who together confess Christ, support one another, and stand firm against temptation together.

But one thing more needs to be said about the corporate nature of Holy Communion. Not only do we share a joy as we commune together with our family, our friends, and our fellow church members, but there is also a mystical fellowship with all those of our family and friends who have died "in the Lord" that is heightened at the moment we commune.

Have you ever been in some of the old rural churches where there is a little semicircular communion rail going halfway around the altar? Did you know that the semicircle is mystically completed in communion as it continues around the altar and up around the throne of God in heaven at that moment when we chant, "with angels and archangels and with all the company of heaven": "Holy, holy, holy Lord, God of Sabaoth. Heaven and earth are full of your glory."

Just listen! You can hear them singing with you—the angels of heaven, the great saints of ages past, your grandparents, or your parents or the spouse or brother or sister or the child you lost. At the moment you commune, you are swept together with them into one great host, rejoicing and praising God and saying: "Hosanna in the highest. Blessed is he who comes in the name of the Lord. Hosanna in the highest."

They are not dead. They are "with the Lord." And we, united with them, endlessly praise His holy name.

So there you have the joyful communion. Intensely *personal*—you are penetrated by your Savior. Intensely *corporate*—you are bound together with others here and others there in a living, loving Christ.

So come, you who are blessed by our heavenly Father! Inherit and feast on the heavenly banquet prepared for you since the creation of this world (Matt. 25:34).

Lent: A Time for Renewal of Faith

[We] are justified freely by his grace through the redemption that came by Christ Jesus. God presented him as a sacrifice of atonement, through faith in his blood. (Rom. 3:24–25)

[The preacher can focus on a variety of applications on the basis of the Romans passage. Aho's classic outline is one approach. I offer another, stemming from some of the insights in his three sections under "An Examination of Renewal in Relation to Faith." Some of my material is to be credited to Edwin C. Munson in *The Cross* (Augsburg, 1936—direct quotes or adaptation).]

Introduction

A pastor in the Pacific Northwest tells of the dramatization of Christ's trial and crucifixion by the youth group at his church. The youth director played the role of Christ, the youth the jeering mob.

"Crucify him! Crucify him!" they shouted, and then they dragged the youth director into the back yard of the church and hung him up on an improvised cross.

The pastor stood to the side of the assembly to "see how the drama was going." The youth were hushed now, as "Christ" hung there and spoke these words to the youth group: "Even though you are doing this to me, I still love you."

And then the pastor noticed an eight-year-old girl standing in the front of the group, transfixed by the scene. He looked at her and saw real tears streaming down her face.

"And," the pastor stated, *"I was envious of her.* For us 'professionals' it was a 'performance.' For her, it was the real thing. *She was there."*

So often you and I come to a Good Friday service and merely *observe* what is happening to Christ. We are uninvolved *spectators.* And yet the Savior of the world is hanging there, suffering and dying for your and my sins on the cross.

If you have ever watched a ship go through some locks on its way up a river, you know that it always enters the lock at a low level. The lower gate is then closed, and the water from the upper river is permitted to flow into the lock. The ship rises higher and higher until it is on a level with the river above the dam. Only then can the ship go on with its journey up the river.

What the lock is for the ship, Lent should be for the Christian. Lent receives you at a low spiritual level, but it floods you with such peace and pardon and power that it lifts you up and sends you forth on a higher level in your Christian life. Lent seeks to lift you from where you are to where you should be, from sin to salvation, from spiritual lethargy to spiritual vitality—to *a renewed faith*.

Our text for tonight capsulizes that faith: "[We] are justified freely by his grace through the redemption that came by Christ Jesus. God presented him as a sacrifice of atonement, through faith in his blood" (Rom. 3:24–25). If you have come closer to Christ and His cross during Lent, particularly during your worship here this Good Friday night, then the purpose of this sacred season will be fulfilled in your life.

As you contemplate the cross this Good Friday, see this Savior and this salvation. *And so that in faith you may more clearly see your Redeemer as He finishes His walk on the Way of Sorrows, may these four elements mark your worship: detachment, decision, discipline, and devotion.*

I

First, *detachment.* This harried, hurried world of ours sorely needs time for contemplation. Scripture says, "Don't let the world around you squeeze you into its own mold" (Rom. 12:2 Phillips), and yet so many of us followers of the Master are letting just that happen in our lives. We live too much for the temporal and the seen, forgetting that it dims our vision of heaven and the goal toward which we run. As Wordsworth said:

> *The world is too much with us;*
> *Late and soon, getting and spending,*
> *We lay waste our powers.*

This Good Friday should be a time when you can withdraw from the tensions of life for an hour to develop poise and power for the Gethsemanes that lie ahead in your life. Christ prepared for Calvary by secluding Himself from the world to commune with His heavenly Father. Now if He needed detachment from the world to prepare for His great ordeal, how much more don't you need that preparation! This hour should be one step toward fulfilling that need in your life.

Good Friday invites you to pause so that you and your Lord, you and your peace, you and your power in Christ, may again be united. May your faith tonight bring detachment from the world so that, as our Lord often did in His life, you may "come apart and rest awhile."

II

But this detachment should have a purpose—*a renewed faith* in the crucified Christ. And that means having more than just knowledge *about* Christ, *about* being "justified by grace as a gift." It involves a *decision,* empowered by the Holy Spirit, to *live* in the light of that faith.

During Passion Week, some Greeks approached Philip, saying, "We would like to see Jesus." Well, they saw Him all right—suspended from a cross. We may doubt whether they realized what was happening as they saw Him hanging there between two thieves—just as countless millions around us today fail to see in the crucified Jesus the One who holds in His hands the answer to their eternal life or eternal death.

How vital it is that we, who have by the Holy Spirit *decided* our lives for Christ, bring the blessed Gospel of "grace as a gift" to those who by their lives of indifference are daily deciding against Him!

Napoleon used to say, "In every battle there is a crisis, ten or fifteen minutes only, on which the outcome depends. To make proper use of this short space of time means victory; its neglect, defeat!"

So it is in the battle of your life. A prompt and proper decision often decides a destiny. If you neglect the development of your talents, it can be disastrous. Victory or defeat in your life frequently hangs on the thin thread of a seemingly insignificant opportunity.

So consider the opportunities you may have in your life to tell others about "the redemption that came by Christ Jesus." On this Good Friday night, will you decide, quickened by the Holy Spirit, to speak for Christ more openly, more patiently, more persistently? For

> *Jesus calls us o'er the tumult*
> *Of our life's wild, restless sea.*
> *Day by day His sweet voice soundeth,*
> *Saying, "Christian, follow me."*

III

Consider the quality of *discipline* that should mark your renewed life of faith and prepare you for the battles of life to come. Some Christians during Lent practice a short-term "discipline" by eliminating some item from their menu or cutting out some worldly amusement.

Lenten discipline—our Good Friday renewal of faith—must be more thorough than that. Good discipline (and obedience, as we heard in an earlier Lenten service) must precede victory. Those of you athletically inclined know that you don't win by your effort in the contest alone but because of the long months of training that come before the actual contest.

How can you expect to resist a great temptation in the future when you yield to small temptations right now day after day? How can you expect to enjoy the companionships and happiness of heaven if you shun the companionships of Christ's disciples here and seek joy in places and pleasures where Christ is never found?

As followers of the crucified Christ, we are to live in the world but not be filled with it. A ship lives in the water, but if the water gets into the ship, the ship goes to the bottom. So you are to live in the world, but if the world takes possession of you, the ship of your life will sink.

Now discipline is not the heart of Lent and Good Friday; *Christ* is. You will miss the purpose of our whole Lenten pilgrimage toward renewal if you encourage discipline *for its own sake.* Note the words of our text: "[We] are justified *freely* by his grace." It is a *gift.* Discipline is only a means to an end—the life of sanctification that the Holy Spirit works within us. The end is to be a "little Christ" (Luther)—to lead the "Christ-life."

115

IV

The most distinguishing mark of your Christian life is *devotion*. It is the reason for your detachment, the background for your decision, the root for your discipline—all empowered by the Holy Spirit.

As you have faithfully done during Lent, in the days ahead learn time and again from your Savior how to take time for periods of quietude, for mental and spiritual rest and refreshment. Scripture emphasizes this when it says: "Be still, and know that I am God" (Ps. 46:10). "They who wait for the LORD shall *renew* their strength" (Is. 40:31). The implication is that if you can't wait, then you'll have to be satisfied with not having your strength renewed.

May you on this sacred Good Friday night appraise yourself and appreciate your Lord and His dearly won redemptive work for the forgiveness of your sins. May you sigh with the psalmist: "Search me, O God, and know my heart; test me and know my anxious thoughts. See if there is any offensive way in me, and *lead me in the way everlasting*" (Ps. 139:23–24).

Good Friday is a time for renewal of faith—a faith marked by detachment from the world, renewed decision for Christ, self-discipline, and devotion in total faithfulness to Him.

So lift your eyes to the cross and ponder its meaning. Here is One dying willingly for the sins that you willingly committed against Him—today, this past week, all the days of your life. Christ is dying for your sins. How can you ever fully know what that means? And yet by the Holy Spirit's guidance and blessing you can move ahead tonight and through all the days to come into an ever more deeply renewed faith in God's solemn promise and benediction: "You are justified freely by [God's] grace through the redemption that came by Christ Jesus. God presented him as a sacrifice of atonement, through *faith* in his blood."

Easter: A Time for Renewal of Hope

Put your hope in the LORD, *for with the* LORD *is unfailing love and with him is full redemption. (Ps. 130:7)*

[Berthold von Schenk once said: "It is easier to change a doctrine than a tradition." Your people might not be willing to implement Kapfer's suggestions for Easter morning (darkened chancel, etc.), but I certainly urge that you try his insightful approach.

I have sought to lay out the following material so it can be used either way. As you will note, the sermon is almost wholly Kapfer's uplifting message.]

Introduction

An Orthodox priest in Europe was hurrying to his 8:00 a.m. Easter service. His car broke down. In desperation he rushed to a phone and dialed the operator for help. Filled with the joy of Easter morning and without thinking, he greeted the operator with the traditional Easter greeting: "Christ is risen!"

The operator, stunned, replied, "Oh, did he *really?*"

That's the way much of the world responds to Easter this morning: "Oh, did He *really* rise from the tomb? SO WHAT?"

Do you feel that way at all this morning? Oh, you here today believe that Christ did rise. But when you look at the pain, the misery, the unfulfilled hopes and dreams in your life, are you in your heart of hearts inclined to say about the Easter message: "SO WHAT?"

Maybe you feel like the women who went to the tomb on Easter morn. They had lost hope and were despairing also. They were carrying ointments and spices, expecting only to prepare in a less hurried and more thorough manner the body of their dear Master for the sleep of death.

So we go with the women to the tomb this morning, expecting not the surprise of joy but the gloom of defeat and death and hopelessness. And with them we can then experience "Easter: A Time for Renewal of Hope."

I

The triumph of Easter morning began in defeat. That gloom and defeat and hopelessness and death were ours. Only when we know how hopeless life is in the absence of God, only when we know how deadly life is without the living God, only when we know how truly tragic life is without the joy of resurrection, will we know how to live in joyous, lively hope. Peter writes, "Praise be to the God and Father of our Lord Jesus Christ! In his great mercy he has given us new birth into a living hope through the resurrection of Jesus Christ from the dead" (1 Peter 1:3). That living hope is ours. But first we must go with the women to the tomb, not expecting the surprise of joy but the gloom of defeat and death and hopelessness.

Out of the Depths

The prayer of the psalmist from Psalm 130 could easily have been the prayer on the lips of Jesus' followers on Holy Saturday and Easter morning. You who have stood at an ending, at a death—physical or emotional—can understand this prayer:

> *Out of the depths I cry to you, O* LORD;
> *O Lord, hear my voice.*
> *Let your ears be attentive*
> *to my cry for mercy. (Ps. 130:1–2)*

The disciples of Jesus had seen heights and depths. They had seen how high love is, for Jesus had stooped down to the crippled and hurting, the rejected and outcast, and lifted them up. They had seen how high hope could be, for He had told them of the kingdom of God, and He had promised them that "in my Father's house are many rooms" (John 14:2). They had seen how high they could stand, for He had pointed them to the lilies and birds of contentment, the basin and towel of service, and the arms of God that beckoned to them. They caught a glimpse of how high *high* is when Jesus was transfigured.

When you have been on the heights, anything less is low indeed. Now their Lord of hope was laid low in death. Those were the depths—the depths of love conquered, hope dashed, promises withdrawn, and death a certainty. Most of all, if God could not bring hope, if the sinless Son of God could not conquer, how could they? His death was the death of hope. Now evil would become accepted, struggles would be meaningless. Life would not only be under the control of the conquering evil one; it would be out of control with no direction, no purpose, no hope, no reason to fight back.

The entire theme of our Lenten series on renewal would be a farce if Jesus Christ had only died on the cross and were still in a sealed tomb. Renewal cannot happen if the One who came to bring the renewal is just like anyone else, placed into a tomb, conquered by the old enemy, death.

The psalmist did not give up, even in the depths, for "out of the depths" he was reaching up to the God who is there. "O Lord, hear my voice. Let your ears be attentive to my cry for mercy" (Ps. 130:2).

Keeping a Record of Sins

But the psalmist's cry is also one of *repentance.*

The picture of keeping a record of sins is of someone with a ledger who marks down every sin that we have committed. The One who marks is not convinced by our rationalizations, nor is He impressed by our excuses. The One who marks the ledger knows the secret we try to avoid—that we sin against God, that we are accountable to the Holy One.

The hymn writer is correct as he takes us to the cross, points, and declares:

"You who think of sin but lightly, or suppose the evil great, here may view its nature rightly, here its guilt may estimate."

The Lord is the One who knows. Without the cross the ledger stands, and we are condemned. "If you, O LORD, kept a record of sins, O Lord, who could stand?" (v. 3). No one! But . . .

II
But . . .

The little word *but* makes all the difference. It contains the great reversal: forgiveness. The Lord takes the ledger and hands it to His Son. It becomes a bitter cup that Jesus grasps in Gethsemane and takes it where we deserve to be—to the cross. In our place Jesus is tried and declared to be guilty— not of His sins but of ours. The innocent One bears our punishment in His own body on the cross, and He dies there for our sins.

Now God has the ledger in His hands. He grasps it as if to tear it apart from top to bottom, like the curtain in the temple that was torn on Good Friday. But we cannot be sure that He has done it, for Jesus lies in the tomb, and there is no life and forgiveness if there is no life in Him. Only if He can conquer death can we be sure that He has conquered sin and Satan. It is not time yet for the lights to come on and for Easter to begin. We must wait and hope.

Wait and Hope

The psalmist writes, "I wait for the LORD, my soul waits, and in his word I put my hope. My soul waits for the Lord more than watchmen wait for the morning, more than watchmen wait for the morning" (vv. 5–6). If Christ is not raised, life is over—forever. Then the grave is the final destination in life, and utter separation from God is the certainty of eternity. Then we hope in vain at the death of a loved one or our own death. Then the wars and bloodshed and cruelty that abound will only get worse, and there will be no end to them. There is no power, no reason, to struggle against them. Then the best that we can leave our children is tap-dance lessons, sports abilities, college educations, and our money when we die—nothing more, for there would be nothing more. Then life would be lived as too often it is lived—as though Jesus did not rise from the dead.

But if the tomb is empty when the women arrive, then the things to come are already ours, and life is lived far differently. We have a living hope that *agapē* love must and can be lived; that the grave is only a way station on the path to eternal life; that we can call the evil of war and bloodshed what they are—evil and wrong—and never rest until the hope for the peace of God is realized; that there is nothing more important to be shared with our children than the living faith of Easter hope; that life is as new and fresh as the forgiveness of sins, the cleansing of grace, and the power of the risen Christ.

So we approach the tomb with the women at the dawning of a new day, hoping beyond hope and saying, "I wait for the LORD, my soul waits, and in his word I put my hope."

Then we hear the proclamation from an empty tomb with the stone rolled aside: "He is not here! He is risen!" The sound we heard on Good Friday like the tearing of a curtain separating us from God, like a ledger being torn to pieces in the hands of God, is the sound of grace and forgiveness. He is risen! He conquered sin in His body. He conquered Satan. He conquered even death.

At the open tomb hope dawns—not wishful thinking, not empty dreaming, but the living hope in the living Lord. Out of every death—the death called sin or failure or lost opportunities—life can be restored. Out of every evil God still is in control, opening up the future for those who trust in Him. Out of every grave of those who die in Christ life eternal shall arise.

"O Israel, put your hope in the LORD, for with the LORD is unfailing love and with him is full redemption" (v. 7). He has redeemed us by the cross and open tomb. He is risen! And we are raised with Him now. We live in a hope that has not and shall not be conquered by any power.

Now let the lights come on in your life, and live in the light! Now let the cross be unveiled, for it is a glorious cross of forgiveness! Now let the banners be raised in your life of faith! Now let the lilies of joy trumpet the sound of praise to God: He is risen! Hallelujah! Hope is renewed forever and ever!

LENT
A Time for Renewal

WORSHIP RESOURCES

Lent: A Time for Renewal

Worship Resources

These worship resources follow the themes developed in the sermon studies and sample sermons:

Ash Wednesday—*Lent: A Time for Renewal of Servanthood*
Lent 2—*Lent: A Time for Renewal of Obedience*
Lent 3—*Lent: A Time for Renewal of Witness*
Lent 4—*Lent: A Time for Renewal of True Religion*
Lent 5—*Lent: A Time for Renewal of Priorities*
Lent 6—*Lent: A Time for Renewal of Godly Fear*
Maundy Thursday—*Lent: A Time for Renewal of Christian Unity*
Good Friday—*Lent: A Time for Renewal of Faith*
Easter—*Easter: A Time for Renewal of Hope*

Due to the reflective nature of the season, the liturgies for Lent are simple in form. In keeping with the character of the services, it is suggested that the organ or other instrumental music be used only to support the singing. Preludes, postludes, and elaborate hymn introductions may be omitted.

The *Lutheran Worship Agenda* also contains suggested orders of service for use on Ash Wednesday, Maundy Thursday, and Good Friday. *Creative Worship for the Lutheran Parish* gives further suggestions for appropriate hymns, prayers, litanies, and other worship activities. The pastor and worship planners of each congregation will be in the best position to choose worship forms appropriate to the season, the message for the service, and the individual character of the congregation.

The Holy Week and Easter services are joined with the Lenten series of services so that the services for Lent and Holy Week link together events in the life of Christ as preparation for and as celebration of the mighty acts of God for our redemption.

Worship Resources

Ash Wednesday

Lent: A Time for Renewal of Servanthood

The Opening Hymn "Jesus, Refuge of the Weary" (*LW* 90; *TLH* 145; LBW 93)

The Introit of the Day

The Collect

P: Almighty and everlasting God, because you hate nothing you have made and forgive the sins of all who are penitent, create in us new and contrite hearts that we, worthily repenting our sins and acknowledging our wretchedness, may obtain from you, the God of all mercy, perfect remission and forgiveness; through Jesus Christ, your Son, our Lord, who lives and reigns with you and the Holy Spirit, one God, now and forever.

C: **Amen**

Special Music (optional)

The Scripture Reading John 13:1–17

(In times of stress and fear, people turn in on themselves and serve their own needs. The Lord steps into our lives, stills our fears, and teaches us to be foot washers. In the splashing water of his love, he renews our understanding of the greatness of servanthood.)

Scripture Response Based on the Prophet Isaiah

P: The Spirit of the LORD is on him, because the LORD has anointed him to preach good news to the poor, to bind up the brokenhearted, to proclaim freedom for the captives, and release from darkness for the prisoners;

C: **To comfort all who mourn in Zion—to give them a crown of beauty instead of ashes, the oil of gladness instead of mourning, and a garment of praise instead of a spirit of despair.**

P: Surely he took up our infirmities and carried our sorrows;

C: **Yet we considered him stricken by God, smitten by him, and afflicted.**

P: But he was pierced for our transgressions, he was crushed for our iniquities;

C: **The punishment that brought us peace was on him, and by his wounds we are healed.**

P: We all, like sheep, have gone astray; each of us has turned to his own way;

C: **And the LORD has laid on him the iniquity of us all.**

P: He was oppressed and afflicted, yet he did not open his mouth;

C: **He was led like a lamb to the slaughter—how like a lamb, the very Lamb of God, who takes away the sin of the world—**

P: And as a sheep before its shearers is silent,

C: **So he did not open his mouth.**

P: By oppression and judgment he was taken away. And who can speak of his descendants? For he was cut off from the land of the living;

C: **For the transgression of my people he was stricken.**

P: He was assigned a grave with the wicked, and with the rich in his death,

C: **Though he had done no violence, nor was any deceit in his mouth.**

P: That is why Lent begins on this Ash Wednesday with ashes of repentance,

C: **And with the hope of life out of the ashes;**

P: With the Lord Jesus in his suffering, humiliation, agony, and bloody sweat,

C: **And at a cross, where he took our sins on himself, to give us his righteousness.**

All: **That great exchange—God's mercy and forgiveness purchased at the cost of his own son! For God so loved the world that he gave his one and only Son, that whoever believes in him shall not perish but have eternal life. Amen.**

The Sermon Hymn "O God of Mercy, God of Light" (*LW* 397; *TLH* 439; LBW 425)

The Ash Wednesday Message "Lent: A Time for Renewal of Christian Servanthood" — Matthew 20:26

The Offertory

The Ash Wednesday Prayer

P: Lord Jesus, our Servant King, you spoke to us by saying, "You know that the rulers of the Gentiles lord it over them, and their high officials exercise authority over them. Not so with you. Instead, whoever wants to become great among you must be your servant,

C: **"And whoever wants to be first must be your slave—just as the Son of Man did not come to be served, but to serve, and to give his life as a ransom for many."**

P: We confess to you, Lord Jesus, that we are often afraid to be servants of one another.

C: **How will it look, getting up from the table, taking a basin of water and a towel, and washing the feet of other disciples? Serving others in humility goes against my self-created esteem.**

P: We are afraid to be servants, Lord. We have tried it occasionally in the past, and we remember the surprise on some faces—"You're washing my feet?"—the haughty look on others—"Oh, yes, you, the foot washer."

C: **We are afraid of criticism. And we are afraid of what servanthood will cost us:**

P: Self-respect, time, losing our place, losing out, losing. How will it look, Lord?

C: **"Jesus knew that the Father had put all things under his power, and that he had come from God and was returning to God; so he got up from the meal, took off his outer clothing, and wrapped a towel around his waist. After that he poured water into a basin and began to wash his disciples' feet, drying them with the towel that was wrapped around him."**

P: *That's* what it looks like! It looks like Jesus, bending down into our lives, taking the form of a servant, and loving us, even to his death on the cross.

C: **This is what it looks like: "Whatever you did for one of the least of these brothers of mine, you did for me."**

P: This is what it looks like: to be free of fear in the freedom of Christ, to be freed up to serve in the name of the Lord, to be renewed and have the same attitude as that of Christ Jesus:

C: **"Who, being in very nature God, did not count equality with God something to be grasped, but made himself nothing, taking the very nature of a servant, being made in human likeness.**

P: "And being found in appearance as a man, he humbled himself and became obedient to death—even death on a cross! Therefore God exalted him to the highest place and gave him the name that is above every name,

C: **"That at the name of Jesus every knee should bow, in heaven and on earth and under the earth, and every tongue confess that Jesus Christ is Lord, to the glory of God the Father."**

The Confession

All: **We confess to you, Lord Jesus Christ, that we hang on to our selfish pride and boastful vanity and thus have sinned against you by thought, word, and deed. Bend down to us, Lord Jesus,** and by your holy Passion, death, and resurrection free us from sin and enable us to serve.

The Declaration of Grace

P: Beloved in Christ: Our Lord Jesus Christ heard the prayer of our soul. He came to live among us. He stooped down to wash the feet of his disciples, taking on himself the task of a slave. He stooped down in order to be lifted up to a cross, taking on himself the sins of the world. Your sins became his and are forgiven. In exchange, his life became yours by faith so you might be sent as he was sent—to serve.

The Lord's Prayer

The Consecration

The Distribution of the Holy Communion

The Communion Hymns "Lord Jesus, Think on Me" (*LW* 231; *TLH* 320; *LBW* 309)

"I Come, O Savior, to Your Table" (*LW* 242; *TLH* 315; *LBW* 213)

"All Hail the Power of Jesus' Name" (*LW* 272; *TLH* 339; *LBW* 328)

The Closing Prayer

The Benediction

The Recessional Hymn "Let Us Ever Walk with Jesus" (*LW* 381; *TLH* 409; *LBW* 487)

Lent 2

Lent: A Time for Renewal of Obedience

The Opening Hymn "To You, Omniscient Lord of All" (*LW* 234; *TLH* 318; *LBW* 310)

The Order of Vespers (may be chanted)

P: O Lord, open my lips,

C: **And my mouth will declare your praise.**

P: Make haste, O God, to deliver me;

C: **Make haste to help me, O Lord.**

Glory be to the Father and to the Son and to the Holy Spirit; as it was in the beginning, is now, and will be forever. Amen.

Praise to you, O Christ, Lamb of our salvation.

The Psalm 91 (*LW*, pp. 336–37; *TLH*, p. 143; *LBW*, p.258)

Special Music (optional)

The Scripture Reading Mark 14:32–42

(In the Garden of Gethsemane the powers of darkness reached out to Jesus to beckon him away from his divine purpose. Jesus prayed, "Not what I will, but what you will," and then obeyed the Father's will. He renews our hearts in this time of Lent and teaches us obedience to God's calling.)

The Scripture Responses

P: "Going a little farther, he fell on the ground and prayed that if possible the hour might pass from him."

C: **We cannot fathom all that happened that night in Gethsemane, but we do know that the powers of evil were gathering around, ready to destroy the Lord of life. The hour of confrontation between God and evil was now here, and it was focused on this one man, Jesus Christ.**

P: " '*Abba*, Father,' he said."

C: **These are the words of childlike trust and dependence; the words he taught us to say when we pray, "Our Father"; the words that we can say only when we know the Father through his Son.**

P: "Everything is possible for you."

C: **"Thine is the kingdom and the power and the glory." We pray this almost casually, often thoughtlessly. Now Jesus prays for us. Will the Father have some other plan for our salvation? Did**

God have to go this far—even to the point of death?

P: "Take this cup from me."

C: **The cup of bloodshed and violence, of injustice and cruelty; the cup of ugly thoughts, cutting words, shameful deeds; the cup of human rebellion and disobedience; the cup of the creatures setting themselves above the Creator—should the sinless One drink the cup of wrath? Shouldn't we—and then die eternally?**

P: "Yet not what I will."

C: **"Yet"—that word turns everything around in the plan of God. We are disobedient . . . yet! We are all sinners . . . yet! We deserve eternal death . . . yet!**

P: "But what you will."

C: **"Christ died for sins once for all, the righteous for the unrighteous, to bring you to God."**

P: This is why we are here tonight, O Lord. We need to be renewed in our obedience.

C: **Save us, O Lord. Open my lips, and my mouth will declare your praise!**

The Hymn "May We Your Precepts, Lord, Fulfill" (*LW* 389; *TLH* 412; *LBW* 353)

The Sermon "Lent: A Time for Renewal of Obedience" — 1 Peter 5:6

The Offering

The Magnificat (or other appropriate hymn—*LW*, pp. 228–30; *TLH*, p. 43; *LBW*, p. 147)

The Kyrie (*LW*, p. 231; *TLH*, p. 44; *LBW*, pp. 148-151)

The Prayer for Renewal of Obedience

P: Lord Jesus, during the days of your life on earth, you offered up prayers and petitions with loud cries and tears to the one who could save you from death, and you were heard because of your reverent submission. Although you are the Son, you learned obedience from what you suffered and, once made perfect, you became the source of eternal salvation to all who obey you.

C: **"For just as through the disobedience of the one man the many were made sinners, so also through the obedience of the one man the many will be made righteous." Lord, renew us for obedience.**

P: Being found in human form, you humbled yourself and became obedient to death—even death on a cross.

C: **"For just as through the disobedience of the one man the many were made sinners, so also through the obedience of the one man the many will be made righteous." Lord, renew us for obedience.**

P: "Does the Lord delight in burnt offerings and sacrifices as much as in obeying the voice of the Lord? To obey is better than sacrifice, and to heed is better than the fat of rams."

C: **"For just as through the disobedience of the one man the many were made sinners, so also through the obedience of the one man the many will be made righteous." Lord, renew us for obedience.**

P: People who look intently into the perfect law that gives freedom, and continue to do this, not forgetting what they have heard but doing it—they will be blessed in what they do.

C: **"For just as through the disobedience of the one man the many were made sinners, so also through the obedience of the one man the many will be made righteous." Lord, renew us for obedience.**

P: "Whoever does the will of my Father in heaven is my brother and sister and mother."

C: **"For just as through the disobedience of the one man the many were made sinners, so also through the obedience of the one man the many will be made righteous." Lord, renew us for obedience.**

P: "If you obey my commands, you will remain in my love, just as I have obeyed my Father's commands and remain in his love."

C: **"For just as through the disobedience of the one man the many were made sinners, so also through the obedience of the one man the many will be made righteous." Lord, renew us for obedience.**

P: Lord Jesus, You took the cup of suffering for us in Gethsemane and prayed, "Yet not what I will, but what you will."

C: **Teach us the obedience of seeking the Father's will. Increase our faith so that we may follow his will. Give us the Spirit's power to live in obedience.**

P: Renew us, Lord, for it is time to start again. It is time to see the light more clearly, to walk in the light more accurately, and to delight more fervently in being the children of light.

C: **Jesus Christ, Light of the world, lighten our pathways and empower us each step of the way.**

P: And then, Lord, teach us to pray, obediently and joyfully:

The Lord's Prayer

The Collect

The Benediction

Silent Prayer

Recessional Hymn (optional) "All Praise to Thee, My God, This Night" (*LW* 484; *TLH* 558; *LBW* 278)

Lent 3

Lent: A Time for Renewal of Witness

The Opening Hymn "Come to Calvary's Holy Mountain" (*LW* 96; *TLH* 149; *LBW,* 301)

The Order of Vespers (may be chanted)

P: O Lord, open my lips,

C: And my mouth will declare your praise.

P: Make haste, O God, to deliver me;

C: Make haste to help me, O Lord.

Glory be to the Father and to the Son and to the Holy Spirit; as it was in the beginning, is now, and will be forever. Amen.

Praise to you, O Christ, Lamb of our salvation.

The Psalm 4 (*LW,* p. 314; *TLH,* p. 123; *LBW,* p. 216)

Special Music (optional)

The Scripture Reading Mark 14:66–72

(Peter was accused of being a follower of Jesus. Under the pressure of fear and shock, Peter denied his Lord. Today Jesus would enter the courtyard of our lives to renew our witness to the hope and joy that he has given.)

The Scripture Responses

P: We have been in the courtyard also, Lord, just as Peter was. Opportunities presented themselves to witness to our faith, and like Peter, we were silent.

C: We fear what people will think—that we are fanatics, that we are somehow different. We are different, aren't we, Lord? And yet we hesitate.

P: We hesitate because we don't know what to say. What if we don't say it correctly or we come on too strong? What if they don't agree?

C: We forget to put our trust in you and let your words become our words.

P: And sometimes our witness is lost because our lives speak louder than our words, and no one would guess that we are your followers.

C: At other times our words get in the way of your Word, for we speak angry words or foul words or hurtful words, and then no one will hear the Word of life from our lips.

133

P: This is why we are here tonight, O Lord. We need to be renewed for witness.

C: **Save us, O Lord. Open my lips, and my mouth will declare your praise!**

All: **In Jesus' name. Amen.**

The Hymn "In the Hour of Trial" (*LW* 511; *TLH* 516; *LBW* 106)

The Sermon "Lent: A Time for Renewal of Witness" — Matthew 10:32–33

The Offering

The Nunc Dimittis (or other appropriate hymn—*LW*, pp. 230–31; *TLH*, pp. 43–44; *LBW*, p. 159)

The Kyrie (*LW*, p. 231; *TLH*, p. 44; *LBW*, pp. 148-151)

The Prayer for Renewal of Witness

P: Lord, we pray that you will open our lives so that we may witness to the hope that is in us. Give to us the joyous tongue of a surprised Nathanael, who expressed his faith with the words:

C: **"Rabbi, you are the Son of God; you are the King of Israel."**

P: Give us the humble tongue of John the Baptizer, who pointed away from himself and expressed his faith in the words:

C: **"Look, the Lamb of God!"**

P: Give us the stubbornly insistent tongue of the man born blind, who, in the face of scoffers, expressed his faith with the words:

C: **"Nobody has ever heard of opening the eyes of a man born blind. If this man were not from God, he could do nothing."**

P: Give us the trusting tongue of Martha, who, in spite of grief, expressed her faith with the words:

C: **"Yes, Lord, I believe that you are the Christ, the Son of God, who was to come into the world."**

P: Give us the convinced tongue of Thomas, who laid aside his doubts and expressed his faith with the words:

C: **"My Lord and my God!"**

P: Give us the bold tongue of Peter and John, who, before those who wanted to silence their witness, expressed their faith with the words:

C: **"We cannot help speaking about what we have seen and heard."**

P: Give us also the helping hands of Dorcas, whose expression of faith through selfless serving became a miracle,

C: **And your name was made "known all over Joppa, and many people believed in the Lord."**

P: Help us, Lord, to express our faith

C: **By doing our daily work as something we do for you; by playing in a way that makes a joyful noise to you; by treating our parents, children, spouse, friends, and even our enemies in ways that show your love.**

P: Help us to receive the power to be witnesses, Lord, for we look to the day when

C: **At the name of Jesus every knee should bow, in heaven and on earth and under the earth, and every tongue confess that Jesus Christ is Lord, to the glory of God the Father. Amen.**

The Lord's Prayer

The Collect

The Benediction

Silent Prayer

Recessional Hymn (optional) "O Trinity, O Blessed Light" (*LW* 487; *TLH* 564; *LBW* 275)

Lent 4

Lent: A Time for Renewal of True Religion

The Opening Hymn "Savior, When in Dust to You" (*LW* 93; *TLH* 166; *LBW* 91)

The Order of Vespers (may be chanted)

P: O Lord, open my lips,

C: **And my mouth will declare your praise.**

P: Make haste, O God, to deliver me;

C: **Make haste to help me, O Lord.**

   Glory be to the Father and to the Son and to the Holy Spirit; as it was in the beginning, is now, and will be forever. Amen.

   Praise to you, O Christ, Lamb of our salvation.

The Psalm 126 (*LW,* p. 357; *TLH,* p. 153; *LBW,* p. 280)

Special Music (optional)

The Scripture Readings John 11:45–53; Matthew 26:57–68

(Caiaphas, the high priest, demonstrates a religion so corrupted that instead of revealing and reflecting God, it hides him behind the forms of piety and heartless routine. Lent is the time to renew our understanding of true religion and by the Spirit's power to live it.)

The Scripture Responses

P: We confess, O God, that so often we have misused the freedom of forgiveness that Christ gives and made it into license for our sinful nature, excusing our sins instead of confessing them.

C: **O Lord, have mercy on us.**

P: We too have laid heavy burdens on others—asking of others what you do not ask of us, withholding forgiveness from the penitent or avoiding reconciliation because we would have to back down on our pride.

C: **We too have avoided the weightier matters of religion—justice, mercy, and the sweat of Christian service—and have substituted oiling the machinery of outward religion.**

P: We too have acted as though religion is so private that we can forget the communion of saints and neglect the consolation and upbuilding that happens when we are united in one body in Christ.

C: **We too have the heart of the Pharisees, the Galatians, and the**

Corinthians, and that is why we are here this evening. We need to be renewed for true religion.

All: Save us, O Lord. Open my lips, and my mouth will declare your praise! In Jesus' name. Amen.

The Hymn "Lord of Glory, You Have Bought Us" (*LW* 402; *TLH* 442; *LBW* 424)

The Sermon "Lent: A Time for Renewal of True Religion" — Matthew 23:4

The Offering

The Magnificat (or other appropriate hymn—*LW,* pp. 228–30; *TLH,* p. 43; *LBW,* p. 147)

The Kyrie (*LW,* p. 231; *TLH,* p. 44; *LBW,* p. 148-151)

The Prayer for Renewal of True Religion

P: When we understand, O God, that you hate phoniness and hypocrisy, and that we, like Caiaphas, can use the form of religion as a substitute for the truly religious life, we cry out like the people of Micah's time:

C: **"With what shall I come before the LORD and bow down before the exalted God?**

P: "Shall I come before him with burnt offerings, with calves a year old?

C: **"Will the LORD be pleased with thousands of rams, with ten thousand rivers of oil? Shall I offer my firstborn for my transgression, the fruit of my body for the sin of my soul?"**

P: To them you answered: "He has showed you, O man, what is good. And what does the LORD require of you?

C: **"To act justly and to love mercy and to walk humbly with your God."**

P: It is only in Jesus Christ, the One who came as the just One, the One filled with loving kindness, the humble One, that we have hope for renewal.

C: **Lord of justice, Lord of mercy, Lord of humble obedience, our Lord Jesus Christ, come to us.**

P: By your life of perfect love,

C: **Renew our hearts in true religion.**

P: By your acceptance of insult, beatings, lies, and treachery,

C: **Renew our hearts in true religion.**

P: By your agony and death for us,

C: **Renew our hearts in true religion.**

P: Give us true religion—to worship you with mouth and hand, to serve you in spirit and truth, to take church out of a building and into the world, to be your genuine people of faith and hope and love.

C: **This is our prayer, O Lord, and in Jesus Christ, this is our confidence as we pray:**

The Lord's Prayer

The Collect

The Benediction

Silent Prayer

Recessional Hymn (optional) "Abide with Me" (*LW* 490; *TLH* 552; *LBW* 272)

Lent 5

Lent: A Time for Renewal of Priorities

The Opening Hymn "O Dearest Jesus" (*LW* 119:1–3; *TLH* 143:1–3; *LBW* 123:1–3)

The Order of Vespers (may be chanted)

P: O Lord, open my lips,

C: **And my mouth will declare your praise.**

P: Make haste, O God, to deliver me;

C: **Make haste to help me, O Lord.**

Glory be to the Father and to the Son and to the Holy Spirit; as it was in the beginning, is now, and will be forever. Amen.

Praise to you, O Christ, Lamb of our salvation.

The Psalm 32 (*LW*, pp. 323–24; *TLH*, pp. 130–31; *LBW*, p. 230)

Special Music (optional)

The Scripture Reading John 18:28–19:16

(Buffeted by many pressures, Pontius Pilate bent and then broke, compromising the truth for expediency. We too need to examine our priorities and be renewed in our hearts. Then God will be where he belongs—first and alone in our hearts and lives.)

The Scripture Responses

P: I thought I had done enough. I had given the people the choice between Jesus and Barabbas. I thought that they would surely choose Jesus. Barabbas was an insurrectionist and a robber, stealing from his own people. This Jesus had done nothing—absolutely nothing under Roman law—to warrant death. (*pause*) Lord, help us.

C: **Speak your Word to us, O Lord, for it is time for a renewal of our priorities.**

P: A little blood—that ought to cool their passions and bring sense to the mob. So I ordered the soldiers to scourge Jesus. A little blood wouldn't hurt. That way they would want Jesus released. . . . The soldiers find too much satisfaction in their work. They too are getting out of control. . . . Just a little more blood . . . a little more humiliation—a crown of thorns, a purple king's robe over his bloody shoulders. Now I can take him out to the crowd. It will soon be over for him . . . for them . . . for me. (*pause*) Lord, help us.

C: **Speak your Word to us, O Lord, for it is time for a renewal of our priorities.**

P: I said the right words, didn't I? "Look, I am bringing him out to you to let you know that I find no basis for a charge against him." I did the right thing, didn't I? (*pause*) Lord, help us.

C: **Speak your Word to us, O Lord, for it is time for a renewal of our priorities.**

P: "Here is the man!" That's what I said. I said it loudly, and I pointed. Didn't they see the blood? Why didn't they decide then and there to release him? Instead, they cried out even louder: "Crucify! Crucify!" "*You* take him and crucify him," I said. "As for me, I find no basis for a charge against him." "He must die," they said, "because he claimed to be the Son of God." They were almost out of control. I had to do something. So I spoke to him. He wouldn't answer me. He did not complain. My fear turned to anger over this stubborn Jesus. "Don't you realize I have power either to free you or to crucify you?" I'm not afraid. I have power! (*pause*) Lord, help us.

C: **Speak your Word to us, O Lord, for it is time for a renewal of our priorities.**

P: His answer finally came—something about my having no power unless it had been given from above. Terror began to swell within me. I spoke to the crowd, argued, threatened. Then they charged this Jesus with setting himself up as king in opposition to Caesar. That was true, wasn't it? It didn't matter, I had to act swiftly. (*pause*) Lord, help us.

C: **Speak your Word to us, O Lord, for it is time for a renewal of our priorities.**

P: "Shall I crucify your king?" I asked. "We have no king but Caesar," they shouted. Finally, an admission of loyalty from these rebels! Something good had come out of this. We had both won—they and I. "Take your king and crucify him," I replied. (*pause*) Lord, help us.

C: **Speak your Word to us, Lord. In the midst of temptations and trials, of choices between good and evil, and especially in the gray areas of life; when the pressures mount, and evil argues well for itself, and confusion distorts the truth; in those times, Lord, that are so frequent for your children who must live in the world of evil and compromise and slick lies, speak your Word to us, for it is time for a renewal of our priorities.**

All: **Save us in the name of Jesus Christ, the Righteous One, our Savior and Lord. Amen.**

The Hymn "O Dearest Jesus" (*LW* 119:4–5; *TLH* 143:4–5; *LBW* 123:4–5)

The Sermon "Lent: A Time for Renewal of Priorities" — 1 John 2:17

The Offering

The Nunc Dimittis (or other appropriate hymn—*LW*, pp. 230–31; *TLH*, pp. 43–44; *LBW*, p. 159)

The Kyrie (*LW*, p. 231; *TLH*, p. 44; *LBW*, pp. 148–151)

The Prayer for Renewal of Priorities

P: How we need to be renewed, O Lord, especially in our priorities, for without you as the compass of our lives, we are like children "tossed back and forth by the waves, and blown here and there by every wind of teaching and by the cunning and craftiness of men in their deceitful scheming." Renew our priorities, O Lord, and enable us to say and live the words:

C: **"The LORD is my shepherd, I shall not be in want. . . . He leads . . . he restores . . . he guides me. . . ."**

P: When we are led to offer our families everything except knowledge of you and faith in you; when the things of this world become more important in their lives and ours than the kingdom, renew our priorities, O Lord, and enable us to say and live the words:

C: **"Seek first his kingdom and his righteousness, and all these things will be given to you as well."**

P: When our schedules are so full that we have no time for you and the fellowship of saints; when we use the talents you have given to us for everything and everyone but the fellow members of our Lord's body, renew our priorities, O Lord, and enable us to say and live the words:

C: **"Above all, love each other deeply, because love covers over a multitude of sins. . . . Each one should use whatever gift he has received to serve others, faithfully administering God's grace in its various forms."**

P: When we are pulled into compromise by the desires, passions, and promises of this world, forgive us, Lord. Renew our priorities, and enable us to say and live the words:

C: **"Do not conform any longer to the pattern of this world, but be transformed by the renewing of your mind. Then you will be able to test and approve what God's will is—his good, pleasing and perfect will."**

P: When we are confronted by the temptation to ignore the good and choose the evil; when we find ourselves rationalizing our compromises;

when we have lost our integrity and feel lost and helpless and condemned, forgive us, O Lord. Renew our priorities, and enable us to say
and live the words:

C: "I have been crucified with Christ and I no longer live, but Christ
lives in me. The life I live in the body, I live by faith in the Son
of God, who loved me and gave himself for me."

P: Live in us, O Lord. Bend our wills to your will. Renew us into your
fresh and forgiven people, and renew our priorities that we may delight
to say and live:

C: "For to me, to live is Christ and to die is gain."

The Lord's Prayer

The Collect

The Benediction

Silent Prayer

Recessional Hymn (optional) "Now the Day Is Over" (*LW* 491;
TLH 654; *LBW* 280)

Lent 6

Lent: A Time for Renewal of Godly Fear

The Opening Hymn "Glory Be to Jesus" (*LW* 98; *TLH* 158; *LBW* 95)

The Order of Vespers (may be chanted)

P: O Lord, open my lips,

C: And my mouth will declare your praise.

P: Make haste, O God, to deliver me;

C: Make haste to help me, O Lord.

Glory be to the Father and to the Son and to the Holy Spirit; as it was in the beginning, is now, and will be forever. Amen.

Praise to you, O Christ, Lamb of our salvation.

The Psalm 28 (*LW*, p. 323; *TLH*, p. 129; *LBW*, p. 228)

Special Music (optional)

The Scripture Reading Luke 23:39–43

(A thief on the cross learned what fear of God means. His crucifixion taught him the Law's condemnation. Yet because Jesus was there beside him, he also learned of the love of God and received the gift of Paradise. He died in awe of God's grace. Lent is the time to reverence God and to receive his guarantee of fellowship with him forever.)

The Scripture Responses

P: Come, let us enter the presence of the living God in this evening hour, for he is here to speak to us, to show his love toward us, and to bless us in every way.

C: Your holiness, your might, your searching eye, O Lord, all make us stand back afraid. For we have not been holy and good; we have struggled with sin and failed again and again. We cannot say that we have no sin.

P: We bring you our broken condition, O Lord, for it is time for renewal of our hearts in godly fear—

C: Fear of your wrath when we sin and fall short, so that we do not take our sins lightly,

P: Yet faith to believe that "since the children have flesh and blood," Jesus himself shared in their humanity

C: "So that by his death he might destroy him who holds the power of death—that is, the devil—and free those who all their lives were held in slavery by their fear of death."

P: Then shall our fear be that of reverence and awe because of your grace, and we shall say with confidence:

C: "The LORD is my light and my salvation—whom shall I fear? The LORD is the stronghold of my life—of whom shall I be afraid?"

P: "One thing I ask of the LORD, this is what I seek: that I may dwell in the house of the LORD all the days of my life, to gaze upon the beauty of the LORD, and to seek him in his temple.

C: "For in the day of trouble he will keep me safe in his dwelling; he will hide me in the shelter of his tabernacle and set me high upon a rock."

P: This is why we are here tonight, O Lord. We need to be renewed in godly fear.

C: Save us, O Lord. Open my lips, and my mouth will declare your praise.

The Hymn "Jesus, in Your Dying Woes" (*LW* 112:1–6; *TLH* 180, 181; *LBW* 112:1–6)

The Sermon "Lent: A Time for Renewal of Godly Fear" — Romans 8:15

The Offering

The Magnificat (*LW*, pp. 228–30; *TLH*, p. 43; *LBW*, 147)

The Kyrie (*LW*, p. 231; *TLH*, p. 44; *LBW*, pp. 148–151)

The Prayer for Renewal of Godly Fear

P: Like the thief on the cross, O Lord, we pray to you in this evening hour:

C: Lord, remember me.

P: We remember, Lord, our sins and failings, and we remember that you know all things and that nothing is hidden from your all-seeing eyes or from your all-hearing ears.

C: Lord, remember me.

P: We remember that, although you have forgiven us, we have a hard time forgiving those who have wronged us and a still harder time seeking reconciliation when someone has been hurt by our action. We remember too well, Lord.

C: Lord, remember me.

P: This is why we are like the thief on the cross; our sins nail us down, our failures expose our spiritual nakedness, and we are afraid of your wrath.

C: **We are afraid, O Lord, that you will deal with us as we deserve. We are afraid that you will deal with us as we have dealt with others. We are afraid that we must face you alone, exposed and helpless.**

P: This is why we pray, "Lord, remember me." In that call we are asking:

C: **"Remember, O LORD, your great mercy and love, for they are from of old.**

P: "Remember not the sins of my youth and my rebellious ways;

C: **According to your love remember me, for you are good, O LORD."**

P: "According to your love remember *me.*" Remember not my sins and failures, my stubborn pride and rebellion.

C: **Remember instead your own Son, Jesus Christ, who came to remember us with the mind of mercy and love, who died to remember us with grace and forgiveness, who rose to remember us with cleansing and new beginnings.**

P: Then teach us to remember, Lord, that if you are for us, who can be against us? You did not spare your own Son, but gave him up for us all. We trust that you will also, along with him, graciously give us all things. Lord, remember us that we may remember:

C: **"Who will bring any charge against God's elect? It is God who justifies. Who is he that condemns? Christ Jesus, who died— more than that, who was raised to life—is at the right hand of God and is also interceding for us."**

P: Help us to answer with godly fear that you have forgiven us through Jesus Christ and that no one can condemn us. Then enable us to say:

C: **"I am convinced that neither death nor life, neither angels nor demons, neither the present nor the future, nor any powers, neither height nor depth, nor anything else in all creation, will be able to separate us from the love of God that is in Christ Jesus our Lord."**

P: Lord of mercy and grace, who took to the cross our sins that caused us to walk in dread and fear,

C: **Renew us in godly fear, that we may walk in reverence and awe before you.**

P: Then the pathways shall open before us, and we shall walk with you and say:

C: "Even though I walk through the valley of the shadow of death, I will fear no evil, for you are with me."

The Lord's Prayer

The Collect

The Benediction

Silent Prayer

Recessional Hymn (optional) "Savior, Again to Your Dear Name" (*LW* 221; *TLH* 47; *LBW* 262)

Maundy Thursday

A Time for Renewal of Christian Unity

The Opening Hymn "O Lord, We Praise You" (*LW* 238; *TLH* 313; *LBW* 215)

The Word of Preparation John 13:21–30

The Response to the Word

P: Lord Jesus, we come seeking you on this special evening.

C: **We look for unity with you, for unity within, for unity with others. But we see so much disunity, so much brokenness.**

P: And so did you, Lord, on that evening—the treachery of Judas, the confusion among your disciples and their failure of nerve, the lonely wrestling in the garden, and the events of your Passion that you had known from eternity would come.

C: **We confess our disunity, Lord—our actions and words and thoughts that separate us from you, our own spiritual treacheries and failures of nerve, our distrust of your promises.**

P: Yet in the Upper Room you laid all that aside for a time, and in a wondrous manner you gathered your disciples to yourself by giving yourself in the Sacred Meal.

C: **This is why we are here—to be united with you and with one another as we receive your powerful presence in the bread and in the cup.**

P: As your called and ordained servant of the Word, I proclaim, in the stead and by the command of Jesus, that your sins of separation are forgiven. Jesus gives you his Spirit to bind up your brokenness and make you whole in person and in fellowship.

Special Music (optional)

The Scripture Readings The Old Testament Reading: Psalm 116:12–19

The Epistle: 1 Corinthians 10:16–17

The Holy Gospel: Luke 22:7–20

The Responsive Reading of the Passover Event

P: The Lord said to Moses and Aaron in Egypt:

C: **"This month is to be for you the first month of your year.**

P: "Tell the whole community of Israel that on the tenth day of this month each man is to take a lamb for his family, one for each household.

C: **"If any household is too small for a whole lamb, they must share one with their nearest neighbor, having taken into account the number of people there are.**

P: "The animals you choose must be year-old males without defect, and you may take them from the sheep or the goats.

C: **"Take care of them until the fourteenth day of the month, when all the people of the community of Israel must slaughter them at twilight.**

P: "Then they are to take some of the blood and put it on the sides and tops of the doorframes of the houses where they eat the lambs.

C: **"That same night they are to eat the meat roasted over the fire, along with bitter herbs, and bread made without yeast.**

P: "Do not eat the meat raw or cooked in water, but roast it over the fire—head, legs and inner parts.

C: **"Do not leave any of it till morning; if some is left till morning, you must burn it.**

P: "This is how you are to eat it: with your cloak tucked into your belt, your sandals on your feet and your staff in your hand. Eat it in haste; it is the LORD's Passover.

C: **"On that same night I will pass through Egypt and strike down every firstborn—both men and animals—and I will bring judgment on all the gods of Egypt. I am the LORD.**

P: "The blood will be a sign for you on the houses where you are; and when I see the blood, I will pass over you. No destructive plague will touch you when I strike Egypt.

C: **"This is a day you are to commemorate; for the generations to come you shall celebrate it as a festival to the LORD—a lasting ordinance."**

The Sermon Hymn "The Church's One Foundation" (*LW* 289; *TLH* 473; *LBW* 369)

The Message "Lent: A Time for Renewal of Christian Unity" —

1 Corinthians 10:17

The Offertory

The Prayer for Christian Unity

P: Jesus said: "My prayer is not for them alone. I pray also for those who will believe in me through their message."

C: **O Lord, unite us with you by the words of the prophets and** apostles, so that we are "no longer foreigners and aliens, but fellow citizens with God's people and members of God's household, built on the foundation of the apostles and prophets, with Christ Jesus himself as the chief cornerstone."

P: Jesus prayed "that all of them may be one, Father, just as you are in me and I am in you."

C: **O Lord, unite us with yourself, that we may know whose we are.**

P: Jesus prayed: "May they also be in us so that the world may believe that you have sent me."

C: **Unite us, O Lord, to yourself, that we may with one united body and one voice proclaim your glory and praise.**

P: Jesus said: "I have given them the glory that you gave me, that they may be one as we are one."

C: **Unite us as members of your holy Christian church, O Lord, that we may with one voice proclaim "one Lord, one faith, one baptism, one God and Father of all, who is over all and through all and in all."**

P: Jesus said: "I in them and you in me. May they be brought to complete unity to let the world know that you sent me and have loved them even as you have loved me."

C: **Unite us, O Lord, so that our lives may confess that "whenever you eat this bread and drink this cup, you proclaim the Lord's death until he comes."**

P: Jesus said: "Father, I want those you have given me to be with me where I am, and to see my glory, the glory you have given me because you loved me before the creation of the world."

C: **Unite us, O Lord, that we may celebrate together at the Holy Meal the foretaste of the feast to come.**

All: **Come, Lord Jesus, unite us to yourself that we may be united in faith and fellowship. Amen.**

The Lord's Prayer

The Consecration

The Distribution of the Holy Communion

The Distribution Hymn "Soul, Adorn Yourself with Gladness"
(*LW* 239; *TLH* 305; *LBW* 224)

The Closing Collect

The Benediction

Silent Prayer

Recessional Hymn (optional) "O Jesus, Blessed Lord, My Praise"
(*LW* 245; *TLH* 309; *LBW* 220)

Good Friday

A Time for Renewal of Faith

Silent Meditation

The Opening Hymn "When I Survey the Wondrous Cross" (*LW* 114, 115; *TLH* 175; *LBW* 482)

The Confession at the Cross

P: Beloved in the Lord, on this Good Friday we not only enter this place of worship, but in mind we go to that place called Calvary to kneel beneath the cross.

C: **We have come because we need the renewal of our faith.**

P: Jesus said: "Father, forgive them, for they do not know what they are doing."

C: **Forgive us, Lord, for doing what we should not do and for not doing what we should do.**

P: Jesus said: "I tell you the truth, today you will be with me in paradise."

C: **Forgive us, Lord, for seeking first the things that this world offers, for building our own kingdoms, for our materialism and misplaced priorities, and for neglecting the kingdom you came to bestow.**

P: Jesus said, "Dear woman, here is your son. . . . Here is your mother."

C: **Forgive us, Lord, for neglecting those in need, for ignoring the poor and helpless and hurting, for scorning your call to servanthood.**

P: Jesus said, "My God, my God, why have you forsaken me?"

C: **Forgive us, Lord, for the times that we have turned our backs on your Word, the times when we have gone through trial and have suspected that you weren't there, the times when we weren't there to help and comfort the lowly.**

P: Jesus said, "I am thirsty."

C: **Forgive us, Lord, when we have not thirsted for righteousness and peace and hope and joy and kindness, neglecting the fruit-ful life that the Spirit would bestow.**

P: Jesus said, "It is finished."

C: **Forgive us, Lord, when we have doubted your grace and have tried to add to our salvation by depending on ourselves and what we can do to gain your favor.**

P: Jesus said, "Father, into your hands I commit my spirit."

C: **Forgive us, Lord, for not commending our past failures to your mercy, our present situations to your governance, and our futures to your care. Lord, have mercy on us sinners who in our inner being still delight in your law. Deliver us from this twisted state.**

P: As your called and ordained servant, I proclaim that you are not condemned; you are justified by grace through faith in Christ Jesus. You have been set free from the law of sin and death. Set your mind now on what the Spirit desires. This will give you life and peace and renew your faith.

The Hymn "Christ, the Life of All the Living" (*LW* 94; *TLH* 151; *LBW* 97)

Special Music (optional)

The Scripture Readings The Old Testament Reading: Isaiah 52:13–53:12

The Epistle: Hebrews 4:14–16; 5:7–9

The Holy Gospel: John 19:17–30

The Sermon Hymn "O Sacred Head, Now Wounded" (*LW* 113; *TLH* 172; *LBW* 116)

The Sermon "Lent: A Time for Renewal of Faith" — Romans 3:24–25

The Offertory

The Prayer for Faith

P: Renew our faith, O Lord.

C: **Give us faith to believe that Christ died for our sins.**

P: Renew our faith, O Lord.

C: **Give us faith to believe that only in Christ is there peace with God.**

P: Renew our faith, O Lord.

C: **Give us faith to believe that we have died to sin with Christ and have been raised to a new life.**

P: Renew our faith, O Lord.

C: **Give us faith to believe that your love is boundless, your mercy limitless, your forgiveness as certain as the cross on which you died for us.**

P: Renew our faith, O Lord.

C: Give us faith to believe that we are justified by your grace as a gift, through the redemption that you put forward, an expiation by your blood, to be received by faith.

The Song of Faith "My Faith Looks Trustingly" (*LW* 378; *TLH* 394; *LBW* 479)

The Lord's Prayer

The Benediction

Silent Prayer

Easter

A Time for Renewal of Hope

The followers of Jesus on that first Easter morning came to the tomb expecting nothing more than the final opportunity to prepare Jesus' body for the sleep of death. His burial on Good Friday had been done in haste; now they would be able to take ample time for proper preparation of their beloved Master's body. On this Easter morning, we signal this same mood with the bare chancel, the dimmed lights, and the solemn responses.

The Preservice Responses

P: Throughout the ages, and especially on a Good Friday and Holy Saturday so long ago, the words of grief and defeat have been spoken: "A voice says, 'Cry out.' And I said, 'What shall I cry?' 'All men are like grass, and all their glory is like the flowers of the field. The grass withers and the flowers fall, because the breath of the LORD blows on them. Surely the people are grass.' "

C: **"The grass withers and the flowers fall." Surely we are like the grass. Our futures are blocked by death, especially the death of him who came to save us. Who will roll away the stone of death, the heavy stone that seals our lives in the tomb of spiritual and physical and eternal death?**

P: "The grass withers and the flowers fall, but the word of our God stands forever." And this is the Word of the living God. Let us stand to hear it and receive it.

The Easter Gospel Mark 16:1–6 (The congregation shall rise.)

P: "When the Sabbath was over, Mary Magdalene, Mary the mother of James, and Salome bought spices so that they might go to anoint Jesus' body.

C: **"Very early on the first day of the week, just after sunrise, they were on their way to the tomb and they asked each other, 'Who will roll the stone away from the entrance of the tomb?'**

P: "But when they looked up, they saw that the stone, which was very large, had been rolled away. As they entered the tomb, they saw a young man dressed in a white robe sitting on the right side, and they were alarmed.

157

C: " 'Don't be alarmed,' he said. 'You are looking for Jesus the Nazarene, who was crucified. He has risen! He is not here. See the place where they laid him.' "

The Processional Hymn "Jesus Christ Is Risen Today" (*LW* 127; *TLH* 199; *LBW* 151)

(During the Processional Hymn, the Easter flowers may be brought forward and placed in the chancel, the Easter banner may be displayed, and the altar cross may be unveiled.)

The Kyrie (*LW*, pp. 179–80; *TLH* p. 17; *LBW*, pp. 78–79)

The Hymn of Praise "This Is the Feast" (*LW*, pp. 182–83; *LBW* pp. 81–82) or "Gloria in Excelsis" (*TLH*, pp. 17–19)

The Collect of the Day

The Easter Epistle 1 Corinthians 15:19–28

The Sermon Hymn "I Know That My Redeemer Lives" (*LW* 264:1–6; *TLH* 200:1–6; *LBW* 352:1–6)

The Sermon "Easter: A Time for Renewal of Hope" — Psalm 130:7

The Offertory

Special Music (optional)

The Responsive Prayer for Hope

P: Holy Triune God, on this day of resurrection, we praise your name for the sudden surprise of life from death, for "the stone the builders rejected has become the capstone;

C: "The Lord has done this, and it is marvelous in our eyes. This is the day the Lord has made; let us rejoice and be glad in it."

P: On this happy day of resurrection, O Lord God, give us the hope of sin conquered through the cross of Christ, and teach us to say:

C: "Therefore, since we have been justified through faith, we have peace with God through our Lord Jesus Christ, through whom we have gained access by faith into this grace in which we now stand. And we rejoice in the hope of the glory of God."

P: On this glorious day of new life bestowed, give us hope, O Lord God, the hope of salvation, and teach us to say:

C: "Since we belong to the day, let us be self-controlled, putting on faith and love as a breastplate, and the hope of salvation as a helmet. For God did not appoint us to suffer wrath but to receive salvation through our Lord Jesus Christ. He died for us so that, whether we are awake or asleep, we may live together with him. Therefore encourage one another and build each other up, just as in fact you are doing."

P: On this wondrous day of death conquered through an open, empty tomb, give us hope, O Lord God, the hope of triumph over death, and teach us to say:

C: **"Brothers, we do not want you to be ignorant about those who fall asleep, or to grieve like the rest of men, who have no hope. We believe that Jesus died and rose again and so we believe that God will bring with Jesus those who have fallen asleep in him."**

P: On this blessed day of victory over Satan's powers, give us hope, O Lord God, the hope of eternal life, and teach us to say:

C: **"Praise be to the God and Father of our Lord Jesus Christ! In his great mercy he has given us new birth into a living hope through the resurrection of Jesus Christ from the dead, and into an inheritance that can never perish, spoil or fade—kept in heaven for you, who through faith are shielded by God's power until the coming of the salvation that is ready to be revealed in the last time."**

P: When trials and sufferings rob us of joy and lead us toward hopelessness, give us Easter hope, O God, that we may . . .

C: **". . . rejoice in our sufferings, because we know that suffering produces perseverance; perseverance, character; and character, hope. And hope does not disappoint us, because God has poured out his love into our hearts by the Holy Spirit, whom he has given us."**

P: When we begin to lose our zeal for you, O God, and our spirits grow weary in serving, give us Easter hope that we may know . . .

C: **". . . the hope to which he has called you, the riches of his glorious inheritance in the saints, and his incomparably great power for us who believe. That power is like the working of his mighty strength, which he exerted in Christ when he raised him from the dead and seated him at his right hand in the heavenly realms."**

P: Lord Jesus Christ, you are the conqueror, the victor, the giver of life, for you have conquered sin and death.

C: **We give you our praise and thanksgiving, risen Lord.**

P: Lord Jesus Christ, God of hope, filling us with all joy and peace in believing, so that by the power of the Holy Spirit we may abound in hope,

C: **Renew our servanthood, obedience, witness, religion, priorities, godly awe, unity, faith, and hope. Amen.**

The Liturgy of Holy Communion (*LW,* p. 189; *TLH,* p. 22; *LBW,* p.88)

The Lord's Prayer

The Consecration

The Agnus Dei

The Distribution of the Holy Communion

The Distribution Hymn "Jesus Christ, My Sure Defense" (*LW* 266; *TLH* 206; *LBW* 340)

The Collect

The Benediction

The Recessional Hymn "I Know That My Redeemer Lives" (*LW* 264:7–8; *TLH* 200:7–8; *LBW* 352:7–8)

The Postlude